ARDUINO SUN TRACKING, ROBOTIC ARM, CELL PHONE CONTROLLED ROBOT CAR, PROPELLER DROVE SHOW, AUTOMATIC PLANT IRRIGATION INTERESTING PROJECTS FOR FUTURE ENHANCEMENT.

Arduino Sun Tracking, Robotic Arm, Cell Phone Controlled Robot Car, propeller drove show, Automatic Plant Irrigation interesting projects for future enhancement.

ACKNOWLEDGMENTS

The writer might want to recognize the diligent work of the article group in assembling this book. He might likewise want to recognize the diligent work of the Raspberry Pi Foundation and the Arduino bunch for assembling items and networks that help to make the Internet of Things increasingly open to the overall population. Yahoo for the democratization of innovation!

INTRODUCTION

The Internet of Things (IOT) is a perplexing idea comprised of numerous PCs and numerous correspondence ways. Some IOT gadgets are associated with the Internet and some are most certainly not. Some IOT gadgets structure swarms that convey among themselves. Some are intended for a solitary reason, while some are increasingly universally useful PCs. This book is intended to demonstrate to you the IOT from the back to front. By structure IOT gadgets, the per user will comprehend the essential ideas and will almost certainly develop utilizing the rudiments to make his or her very own IOT applications. These included ventures will tell the per user the best way to assemble their very own IOT ventures and to develop the models appeared. The significance of Computer Security in IOT gadgets is additionally talked about and different systems for protecting the IOT from unapproved clients or programmers. The most significant takeaway from this book is in structure the tasks yourself.

1. ARDUINO WEIGHT MEASUREMENT UTILIZING LOAD CELL AS WELL AS HX711 MODULE

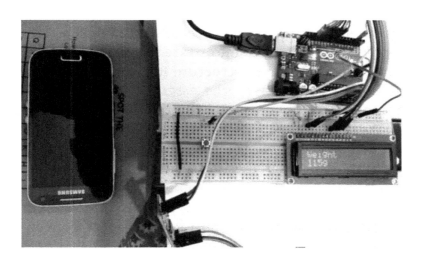

Today we are gonna to Measure the Weight by interfacing Load Cell as well as HX711 Weight Sensor with Arduino. We have seen weight machines at numerous shops, where machine shows the weight just by putting any thing on the gauging stage. So here we are building a similar Weighing machine by utilizing Arduino and Load cells, having limit of estimating upto

40kg. This point of confinement can be additionally expanded by utilizing the Load cell of higher limit.

Required Components:

- Arduino Uno
- Load cell (40kg)
- HX711 Load cell Amplifier Module
- 16x2 LCD
- Connecting wires
- USB cable
- Breadboard
- Nut bolts, Frame and base

Load Cell and HX711 Weight Sensor Module:

Burden cell is transducer which changes power or weight into electrical yield. Extent of this electrical yield is straightforwardly extent to the power being applied. Burden cells have strain check, which misshapes when weight is applied on it. And afterward strain measure produces electrical sign on twisting as its compelling obstruction changes on misshapening. A heap cell more often than not comprises of 4 strain checks in a Wheatstone connect arrangement. Burden cell comes in different reaches like 5kg, 10kg, 100kg and the sky is the limit from there, here we have used Load cell, which can weight upto 40kg.

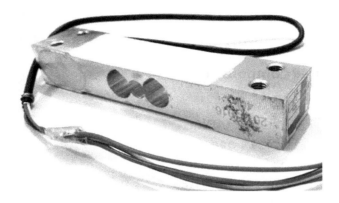

Presently the electrical sign produced by Load cell is in not many millivolts, so they should be further intensify by some enhancer and consequently HX711 Weighing Sensor comes into picture. HX711 Weighing Sensor Module has HX711 chip, which is a 24 high exactness A/D converter (Analog to computerized converter). HX711 has two simple info channels and we can get addition up to128 by programming these channels. So HX711 module intensifies the low electric yield of Load cells and afterward this enhanced and carefully changed over sign is encouraged into the Arduino to determine the weight.

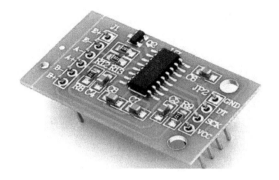

Burden cell is associated with HX711 Load cell Amplifier utilizing four wires. These four wires are Red, Black, White and Green/Blue. There might be slight variety in shades of wires from module to module. Beneath the association subtleties and chart:

- RED Wire is associated with E+

- Dark Wire is associated with E-

- WHITE Wire is associated with A-

- GREEN Wire is associated with A+

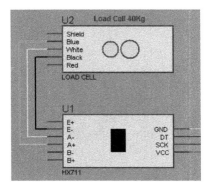

Fixing Load Cell with Platform and Base:

This progression is discretionary and you can legitimately put the loads on the Load cell without Platform and can just brace it without fixing it with any base, yet it's smarter to append a stage for putting the enormous things on it and fix it on a Base so it stop. So here we have to make an edge or stage for putting the things for weight estimation. A base is additionally required to fix the heap cell over it by utilizing stray pieces. Here we have utilized a hard cardboard for the casing for setting things over it and a wooden board as Base. Presently do the associations as appeared in the circuit chart and you are all set.

Circuit Explanation:

Associations for this venture are simple and schematic is given underneath. 16x2 LCD pins RS, EN, d4, d5, d6, and d7 are associated with stick number 8, 9, 10, 11, 12 and 13 of Arduino separately. HX711 Module's DT and SCK pins are legitimately associated with Arduino's stick A0 and A1. Burden cell associations with HX711 module are now clarified before and furthermore appeared in the beneath circuit chart.

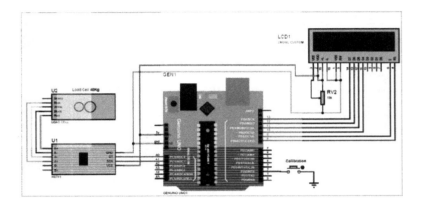

Working Explanation:

Working of this Arduino Weight Measurement venture is simple. Prior to going into subtleties, first we need to adjust this framework for estimating right weight. At the point when client determination it up then framework will consequently begin adjusting. What's more, in the event that client needs to align it physically, at that point press the push button. We have made a capacity void adjust() for alignment reason, check the code beneath.

For adjustment, sit tight for LCD sign for putting 100 gram over the heap cell as appeared in beneath picture. At the point when LCD will show "put 100g" at that point put the 100g load over the heap cell and pause. After certain seconds adjustment procedure will be done. After alignment client may put any weight (max 40kg) over the heap cell and can get the incentive over LCD in grams.

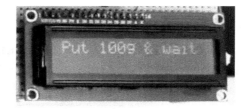

In this task, we have used Arduino to control entire the procedure. Burden cell detects the weight as well as supplies an electrical simple voltage to HX711 Load Amplifier Module. HX711 is a 24bit ADC, which intensifies and carefully changes over the Load cell yield. At that point this enhanced worth is encouraged to the Arduino. Presently Arduino ascertain the yield of HX711 and changes over that into the weight esteems in grams and show it on LCD. A push catch is utilized for aligning the framework. We have composed an Arduino program for entire procedure, check the Code toward the finish of this instructional exercise.

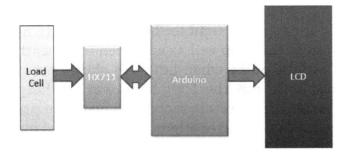

Programming Explanation:

Programming some portion of this venture is minimal complex for tenderfoots. In this venture, we didn't utilize any library for interfacing HX711 load sensor with Arduino. We have quite recently pursued the datasheet of HX711 and application notes. In spite of the fact that there are a few libraries present for this reason, where you just need to incorporate that library and you can get the weight utilizing one line of code.

As a matter of first importance, we have included header document for LCD and characterized the pins for the equivalent. Furthermore, for push button moreover. At that point pronounced a few factors for computation reason.

```
#include <LiquidCrystal.h>

LiquidCrystal lcd(8, 9, 10, 11, 12, 13);
```

```
#define DT A0

#define SCK A1

#define sw 2

long sample=0;

float val=0;

long count=0;
```

After it, we have made underneath work for perusing information from HX711 module and return its yield.

```
unsigned long readCount(void)

{

  unsigned long Count;

  unsigned char i;

  pinMode(DT, OUTPUT);

  digitalWrite(DT,HIGH);

  digitalWrite(SCK,LOW);
```

```
Count=0;

pinMode(DT, INPUT);

while(digitalRead(DT));

for (i=0;i<24;i++)

{

  digitalWrite(SCK,HIGH);

  Count=Count<<1;

  digitalWrite(SCK,LOW);

  if(digitalRead(DT))

  Count++;

}

digitalWrite(SCK,HIGH);

Count=Count^0x800000;

digitalWrite(SCK,LOW);

return(Count);
```

```
}
```

After it, we have instate LCD and offer bearings to information and yield sticks in void arrangement().

```
void setup()

{

  Serial.begin(9600);

  pinMode(SCK, OUTPUT);

  pinMode(sw, INPUT_PULLUP);

  lcd.begin(16, 2);

  lcd.print(" Weight ");

  lcd.setCursor(0,1);

  lcd.print(" Measurement ");

  delay(1000);

  lcd.clear();

  calibrate();
```

```
}
```

Next in void circle() work, we have perused information from HX711 module and changed over this information into weight (grams) and sent it to the LCD.

```
void loop()

{

count = readCount();

   int  w=(((count-sample)/val)-2*((count-sample)/
val));

Serial.print("weight:");

Serial.print((int)w);

Serial.println("g");

lcd.setCursor(0,0);

lcd.print("Weight      ");

lcd.setCursor(0,1);

lcd.print(w);
```

```
lcd.print("g      ");

if(digitalRead(sw)==0)

{

  val=0;

  sample=0;

  w=0;

  count=0;

  calibrate();

}

}
```

Prior to this, we have made an adjustment work in which we have aligned the framework by setting the 100gm load over the Load cell.

```
void calibrate()

{

  lcd.clear();
```

```
lcd.print("Calibrating...");

lcd.setCursor(0,1);

lcd.print("Please Wait...");

for(int i=0;i<100;i++)

{

  count=readCount();

  sample+=count;

  Serial.println(count);

}
.........
.........
```

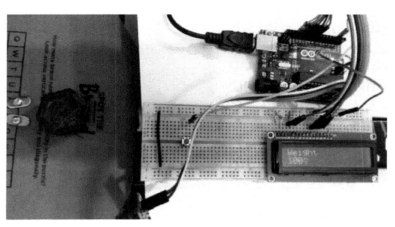

So here we have taken in the essential Interfacing of Load cell and HX11 Weight Sensor with Arduino to gauge the loads. In our content instructional exercises we will make a few applications dependent on weight estimation like Smart compartment, Automatic entryway and so on.

Code

```
#include <LiquidCrystal.h>
LiquidCrystal lcd(8, 9, 10, 11, 12, 13);
#define DT A0
#define SCK A1
#define sw 2
long sample=0;
float val=0;
long count=0;
unsigned long readCount(void)
{
```

```
unsigned long Count;
unsigned char i;
pinMode(DT, OUTPUT);
digitalWrite(DT,HIGH);
digitalWrite(SCK,LOW);
Count=0;
pinMode(DT, INPUT);
while(digitalRead(DT));
for (i=0;i<24;i++)
{
 digitalWrite(SCK,HIGH);
 Count=Count<<1;
 digitalWrite(SCK,LOW);
 if(digitalRead(DT))
 Count++;
}
 digitalWrite(SCK,HIGH);
 Count=Count^0x800000;
 digitalWrite(SCK,LOW);
 return(Count);
}
void setup()
{
 Serial.begin(9600);
 pinMode(SCK, OUTPUT);
 pinMode(sw, INPUT_PULLUP);
 lcd.begin(16, 2);
 lcd.print(" Weight ");
 lcd.setCursor(0,1);
 lcd.print("Measurement ");
```

```
 delay(1000);
 lcd.clear();
 calibrate();
}
void loop()
{
 count= readCount();
    int   w=(((count-sample)/val)-2*((count-sample)/
val));
 Serial.print("weight:");
 Serial.print((int)w);
 Serial.println("g");
 lcd.setCursor(0,0);
 lcd.print("Weight      ");
 lcd.setCursor(0,1);
 lcd.print(w);
 lcd.print("g      ");
 if(digitalRead(sw)==0)
 {
  val=0;
  sample=0;
  w=0;
  count=0;
  calibrate();
 }
}
void calibrate()
{
  lcd.clear();
 lcd.print("Calibrating...");
```

```
lcd.setCursor(0,1);
lcd.print("Please Wait...");
for(int i=0;i<100;i++)
{
 count=readCount();
 sample+=count;
 Serial.println(count);
}
sample/=100;
Serial.print("Avg:");
Serial.println(sample);
lcd.clear();
lcd.print("Put 100g & wait");
count=0;
while(count<1000)
{
 count=readCount();
 count=sample-count;
 Serial.println(count);
}
lcd.clear();
lcd.print("Please Wait....");
delay(2000);
for(int i=0;i<100;i++)
{
 count=readCount();
 val+=sample-count;
 Serial.println(sample-count);
}
 val=val/100.0;
```

```
val=val/100.0;     // put here your calibrating weight
lcd.clear();
}
```

◆ ◆ ◆

2. ARDUINO BASED SUN TRACKING SOLAR PANEL

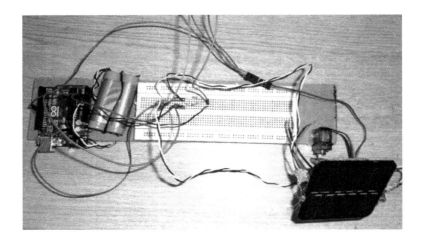

We are gonna to make a Sun Tracking Solar Panel utilizing Arduino, in which we will utilize two LDRs (Light ward resistor) to detect the light and a servo engine to naturally turn the sun powered board toward the daylight. Bit of leeway of this venture is that Solar board will consistently pursue the daylight will consistently look towards the sun to get charge constantly and can give the stockpile the greatest power. The model is anything but difficult to manufacture. Beneath you will locate the total depiction of how it functions and how the model is made.

Required Components:

- Servo Motor (sg90)
- Arduino Uno
- Battery (6 to 12V)
- Sunlight based board
- 10K resistors X 2
- LDR's X 2

How it Works:

In this venture, LDR's are functioning as light finders. Before we broadly expound, we should see how the LDR's work. LDR (Light Dependent Resistor) otherwise called photograph resistor is the light touchy gadget. Its opposition decline when the light falls on it and that is the reason it is every now and again utilized in Dark or Light Detector Circuit. Check the different circuits dependent on LDR here.

The two LDR's are set at the different sides of sun based board and the Servo Motor is utilized to pivot the sun powered board. The servo will move the sun powered board towards the LDR whose obstruction will be low, mean towards the LDR on which light is falling, that way it will continue following the light. What's more, in the event that there is same measure of light falling on both the LDR, at that point servo won't pivot. The servo will attempt to move the sun based board in the position where both LDR's will have a similar obstruction implies where same measure of light will fall on both the resistors and on the off chance that opposition of one of the LDR will change, at that point it pivots towards lower obstruction LDR.

How to Make the Prototype:

To make the model, you should pursue the underneath steps:

Stage 1:

As a matter of first importance, take a little bit of cardboard and make a gap toward one side. We will embed the screw in it to fix it with the servo later on.

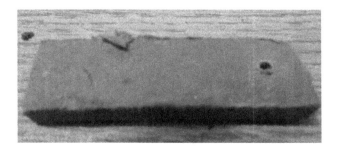

Stage 2:

Presently fix two little bits of cardboard with one

another in a V shape with assistance of paste or hot weapon and spot sun oriented board on it.

Stage 3:

At that point connect the base side of the V shape to the opposite finish of little bit of cardboard in which you made a gap in initial step.

Stage 4:

Presently embed the screw in the gap you made on card board and supplement it through the gap into the servo. The screw accompanies the servo engine when you get it.

Stage 5:

Presently place the servo on another bit of cardboard. The size of the cardboard ought to be bigger enough with the goal that you can put an Arduino Uno, a breadboard and a battery on it.

Stage 6:

Connect the LDRs on the different sides of the sun based board with the assistance of paste. Ensure you have bound the wires with the legs of the LDR's. You should interface these with the resistors later on.

Stage 7:

Presently place the Arduino, battery and the bread-board on the cardboard and make the association as depicted in the Circuit outline and Explanation area beneath. The last model is demonstrated as follows.

Circuit Diagram and Explanation:

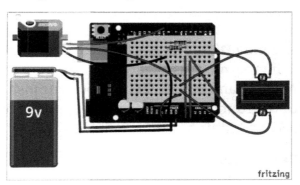

In this Arduino Solar Panel Tracker, Arduino is fueled by the 9V battery as well as the various parts are controlled by the Arduino. Arduino prescribed information voltage is from 7 to 12 volts however you can control it inside the scope of 6 to 20 volts which is the breaking point. Attempt to control it inside the suggested information voltage. So associate the +ve wire of the battery to the Vin of the Arduino and the negative wire of the battery to the ground of the Arduino.

Next associate the servo to the Arduino. Associate the positive wire of the servo to the 5V of Arduino and ground wire to the ground of the Arduino and afterward interface the sign wire of Servo to the computerized stick 9 of Arduino. The servo will help in moving the sun oriented board.

Presently interface the LDRs to the Arduino. Associate one end of the LDR to the one end of the 10k resistor and furthermore interface this conclusion to the A0 of the Arduino and associate the opposite finish of that resistor to the ground and interface the opposite finish of LDR to the 5V. Likewise, interface the one finish of second LDR to the one finish of other 10k resistor and furthermore associate that conclusion to the A1 of Arduino and interface the opposite finish of that resistor to ground and interface the opposite finish of LDR to 5V of Arduino.

Code Explanation:

Code for this Arduino based Solar Panel Tracker is simple and all around clarified by remarks. As a matter of first importance, we will incorporate the library for servo engine. At that point we will instate the variable for the underlying situation of the servo engine. From that point onward, we will introduce the factors to peruse from the LDR sensors and Servo.

```
#include <Servo.h>        //including the library of
servo motor

Servo sg90;              //initializing a variable for servo
named sg90

int initial_position = 90;   //Declaring the initial
position at 90

int LDR1 = A0;           //Pin at which LDR is connected

int LDR2 = A1;           //Pin at which LDR is connected

int error = 5;           //initializing variable for error

int servopin=9;
```

sg90.atach(servopin) order will peruse Servo from the stick 9 of Arduino. Next we set the LDR sticks as information sticks so we can peruse the qualities from the sensors and move the sunlight based board as indicated by that. At that point we set the servo engine at 90 degree which is the underlying situation for the servo.

```
void setup()

{

  sg90.attach(servopin);   // attaches the servo on
  pin 9

  pinMode(LDR1, INPUT);   //Making the LDR pin as
  input

  pinMode(LDR2, INPUT);

  sg90.write(initial_position);   //Move servo at 90
  degree

  delay(2000);            // giving a delay of 2 seconds

}
```

At that point we will peruse the qualities from the LDRs and will spare in R1 and R2. At that point we will take the distinction among the two LDRs to move the servo as needs be. On the off chance that the distinction between them will be zero that it implies that equivalent measure of light is falling on both the LDR's so the sunlight based board won't move. We have utilized a variable named blunder and its worth is 5, the utilization of this variable is that in case the distinction between the two LDRs will be under 5, at that point the servo won't move. In the event that we won't do this, at that point the servo will continue turning. Furthermore, on the off chance that the thing that matters is more prominent than blunder esteem (5) at that point servo will move the sun based board toward the LDR, on which light is falling. Check the Full Code underneath.

```
int R1 = analogRead(LDR1); // reading value from
LDR 1

int R2 = analogRead(LDR2); // reading value from
LDR 2

int diff1 = abs(R1 - R2);   // Calculating the differ-
ence between the LDR's

int diff2 = abs(R2 - R1);

if((diff1 <= error) || (diff2 <= error)) {

    //if the difference is under the error then do
nothing

} else {

    if(R1 > R2)
```

```
{

    initial_position = --initial_position;   //Move
the servo towards 0 degree

}

if(R1 < R2)

{

    initial_position = ++initial_position; //Move
the servo towards 180 degree

}

}
```

So that is the means by which you can assemble a straightforward Solar Panel Tracker, which will consequently move towards the light like a sunflower. Here we have utilized the low control sunlight based board to decrease the weight, on the off chance that you are wanting to utilize a high power or overwhelming sun powered board then you have to pick the Servo engine as needs be.

Code

#include <Servo.h>   //including the library of servo motor

```
Servo sg90;          //initializing a variable for servo
named sg90
int initial_position = 90;  //Declaring the initial posi-
tion at 90
int LDR1 = A0;      //Pin at which LDR is connected
int LDR2 = A1;      //Pin at which LDR is connected
int error = 5;      //initializing variable for error
int servopin=9;
void setup()
{
 sg90.attach(servopin); // attaches the servo on pin 9
  pinMode(LDR1, INPUT);   //Making the LDR pin as
input
 pinMode(LDR2, INPUT);
 sg90.write(initial_position);  //Move servo at 90 de-
gree
  delay(2000);      // giving a delay of 2 seconds
}


void loop()
{
 int R1 = analogRead(LDR1); // reading value from LDR
1
 int R2 = analogRead(LDR2); // reading value from LDR
2
 int diff1 = abs(R1 - R2);  // Calculating the difference
between the LDR's
 int diff2 = abs(R2 - R1);
```

```
if((diff1 <= error) || (diff2 <= error)) {
//if the difference is under the error then do nothing
} else {
if(R1 > R2)
{
    initial_position = --initial_position;  //Move the
servo towards 0 degree
}
if(R1 < R2)
{
    initial_position = ++initial_position; //Move the
servo towards 180 degree
}
}
sg90.write(initial_position); // write the position to
servo
delay(100);
}
```

❖ ❖ ❖

3. SMOKE ALARM UTILIZING MQ2 GAS SENSOR AND ARDUINO

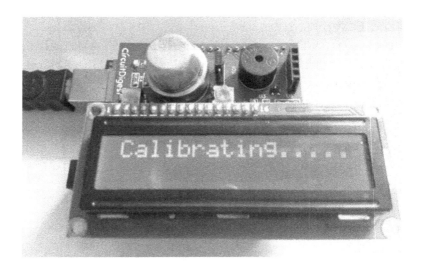

Smoke alarms are valuable in recognizing smoke or fire in structures, as are the significant wellbeing parameters. In this DIY session, we are going to construct a Smoke Detector Circuit which sense the smoke noticeable all around as well as peruses and shows the degree of Smoke in the Air in PPM (parts per million). This circuit triggers the Buzzer when Smoke level gets higher than 1000 ppm, this edge worth can be changed in the Code as indicated by the necessity. This circuit basically utilizes MQ2 Smoke/Gas sensor and Arduino to recognize and ascertain the degree of smoke. MQ2 gas sensor is likewise reasonable to LPG, Alcohol, and Methane and so on.

This Smoke Detector can be effectively based on Bread Board or Dot Board yet we have chosen to construct this as an Arduino Shield on PCB. We have utilized EasyEDA online PCB test system and originator to construct this Smoke Detector Shield for Arduino. We have clarified the entire procedure in this Article and furthermore gave PCB format to this Arduino Shield with the goal that you can likewise arrange this Shield in case you need.

Components Required:

- Arduino UNO
- Smoke Detector Arduino Shield (Self Designed)

- Power Supply

Components for Smoke Detector Arduino Shield:

- Smoke Sensor (MQ2)
- Resistors (10K and 1K)
- Buzzer
- 16x2 LCD
- LED
- 10k POT
- Burg strips
- LM358

Designing Smoke Detector Shield for Arduino:

For planning Smoke Detector Shield for Arduino we have utilized EasyEDA, in which first we have structured a Schematic and afterward changed over that into the PCB format via Auto Routing highlight of EasyEDA.

To configuration circuit and PCB for this Smoke Detector Shield, we picked EasyEDA which is a free online instrument and one stop answer for building up your hardware ventures effortlessly. It offers schematic catch, zest reproduction, PCB configuration for nothing and furthermore offers high caliber yet low value Customized PCB administration. There are countless segment libraries in its editorial manager, so you can without much of a stretch and rapidly locate your ideal parts. Check here the total instructional exercise on How to utilize Easy EDA for making Schematics, PCB designs, Simulating the Circuits and so on.

We have made the Circuit and PCB structure of this Smoke Detector Shield open, so you can simply pursue the connection to get to the Circuit Diagram and PCB formats:

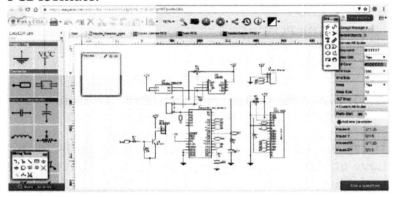

The following is the Snapshot of Top layer of PCB design from EasyEDA, you can see any Layer (Top, Bottom, Topsilk, bottomsilk and so forth) of the PCB by choosing the layer structure the 'Layers' Window.

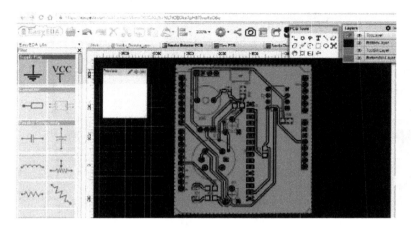

In case you discover any issue in utilizing EasyEDA, at that point look at our recently created 100 watt inverter circuit, where we have clarified the procedure bit by bit.

Ordering the PCB online:

Subsequent to finishing the plan of PCB, you can tap the symbol of Fabrication yield, which will take you on the PCB request page. Here you can see your PCB in Gerber Viewer or download Gerber documents of your PCB and send them to any maker, it's likewise much simpler (and less expensive) to arrange it straightforwardly in EasyEDA. Here you can choose the quantity of PCBs you need to arrange, what number of copper layers you need, the PCB thickness, copper weight, and even the PCB shading. After you have chosen the entirety of the choices, click "Spare to Cart" and complete your request, to get your PCBs inside hardly any days.

Following not many long periods of requesting the PCB, we got our Smoke Detector Arduino Shield PCB, and we found the PCBs in pleasant bundling and the nature of PCB is very amazing.

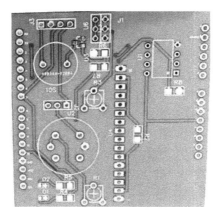

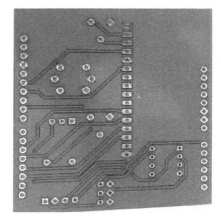

In the wake of getting the PCBs, we have mounted and welded all the necessary segments and burg strips over the PCB, you can have a last look here:

Presently we simply need to append LCD to the Shield and spot this Smoke Detector Shield over the Arduino. Adjust the Pins of this Shield to the Arduino and solidly press it over the Arduino. Presently simply transfer the code to the Arduino and power on circuit and you are finished! Your Smoke Detector is prepared to test.

Circuit Explanation:

In this Smoke Detector Circuit with Arduino, we have utilized a MQ2 Gas Sensor to identify preset smoke noticeable all around. A 16x2 LCD is utilized for showing the PPM estimation of Smoke. Also, a LM358 IC for changing over smoke sensor yield into computerized structure (this capacity is discretionary). A signal is put as a caution which gets activated when smoke level goes past 1000 PPM.

Circuit associations for this venture are straightforward, we have a Comparator Circuit for contrasting yield voltage of smoke sensor and preset voltage (yield associated at stick D7). Additionally smoke sensor yield is associated at a simple stick of Arduino (A0). Ringer is associated at Pin D9. Also, LCD associations are same as Arduino LCD models that are accessible in Arduino IDE (12, 11, 5, 4, 3, 2). Remaining associations are appeared in the circuit graph.

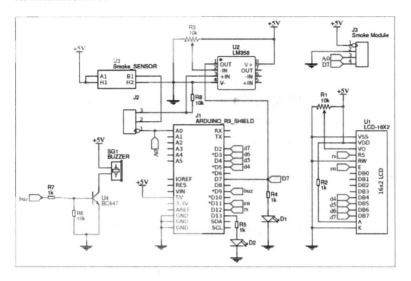

Note: In the circuit we have to short all the three stick of J2 header to compute PPM of smoke.

Programming Explanation:

Program of this venture is minimal hard to make. Client needs to peruse MQ2 Smoke Sensor datasheet cautiously to comprehend the estimations for this undertaking. In this we need to understand slop or bend of smoke fixation in air regarding clean air. Subsequent to perusing datasheet, we get a few esteems that we will require in the Code to compute ppm of smoke in air. Here most of the part we need bend esteems (we take two from the bend), sensor opposition (will be determined in code), clean air steady (9.83) and Load Resistance (I utilized 10K). We can discover bend esteems from the datasheet and we can put load obstruction 5k-54k and afterward we will compute sensor opposition by these worth and smoke tests.

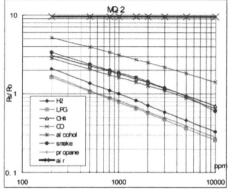

Fig.3 is shows the typical sensitivity characteristics of the MQ-2 for several gases. in their: Temp: 20℃, Humidity: 65%, O₂ concentration 21% RL=5k Ω Ro: sensor resistance at 1000ppm of H₂ in the clean air Rs:sensor resistance at various concentrations of gases.

Take 2 points from the bend as well as take log of them like point one: (lg200, lg3.4)=(2.3,0.53) as well as point 2: (lg10000,lg0.63)=(4,- 0.20). At that point discover incline of the bend utilizing Formula: (y2-y1)/(x2-x1), at that point take one point and slant (-0.44) and use them in the Program (x, y, slant). Further check the Code beneath to comprehend the Calculation.

First we have to incorporate header record for LCD and characterize pins for the equivalent. At that point characterize bend esteems and burden opposition.

```
#include <LiquidCrystal.h>

LiquidCrystal lcd(12, 11, 5, 4, 3, 2);

#define buzzer 9

#define sensor A0

#define load_Res 10

#define air_factor 9.83

float SmokeCurve[3] ={2.3,0.53,-0.44};

float Res=0;
```

Presently in void arrangement(), we have to Calibrate the module by utilizing SensorCalibration work:

```
void setup()

{

  lcd.begin(16,2);

  lcd.print("Calibrating.....");
```

```
Res = SensorCalibration();

lcd.print("Calibration done.");

lcd.setCursor(0,1);

lcd.print("Res=");

lcd.print(Res);

lcd.print("kohm");

delay(2000);

lcd.clear();

pinMode(buzzer, OUTPUT);
}
```

```
float SensorCalibration()

{

int i;

float val=0;
```

```
val=resistance(50,500);

val = val/air_factor;

return val;

}
```

At that point in void circle() work, we have determined the PPM of smoke by utilizing obstruction Function:

```
void loop()

{

  lcd.setCursor(0,0);

  lcd.print("SMOKE:");

  float res=resistance(5,50);

  res/=Res;

  int    result=pow(10,(((log(res)-SmokeCurve[1])/
SmokeCurve[2]) + SmokeCurve[0]));

  lcd.print(result);
```

```
lcd.print("ppm    ");

if(result>1000)

{

    digitalWrite(buzzer, HIGH);

    delay(2000);

}

else

digitalWrite(buzzer, LOW);

delay(500);

}
```

```
float resistance(int samples, int interval)

{

    int i;

    float res=0;
```

```
for (i=0;i<samples;i++)

{

    int adc_value=analogRead(sensor);

    res+=((float)load_Res*(1023-adc_value)/ad-
c_value);

    delay(interval);

}

res/=samples;

return res;

}
```

Note: Before adjusting the module, leave the task for 10 moment in clean air with control On and afterward start the alignment. This alignment procedure will take at any rate 25 seconds.

Locate the total Code beneath.

So here we have assembled the Smoke Detector Circuit utilizing Arduino, which additionally ascertains and shows the degree of the Smoke in PPM. For this Project, we have built up our own Smoke identifier Arduino Shield utilizing EasyEDA PCB structuring administrations, and made those PCB designs Public with the goal that anybody can utilize them to arrange this Smoke Detector Shield.

Code

```
#include <LiquidCrystal.h>
LiquidCrystal lcd(12, 11, 5, 4, 3, 2);
#define buzzer 9
#define sensor A0
#define load_Res 10
#define air_factor 9.83


float SmokeCurve[3] ={2.3,0.53,-0.44};  // (x, y, slope)
```
x,y coordinate of one point and the slope between two points

```
float Res=0;
void setup()
{
lcd.begin(16,2);
lcd.print("Calibrating.....");
          Res       =       SensorCalibration();

lcd.print("Calibration done.");
lcd.setCursor(0,1);
lcd.print("Res=");
lcd.print(Res);
lcd.print("kohm");
```

```
delay(2000);
lcd.clear();
pinMode(buzzer, OUTPUT);
}
void loop()
{
 lcd.setCursor(0,0);
 lcd.print("SMOKE:");
 float res=resistance(5,50);
 res/=Res;
     int   result=pow(10,(((log(res)-SmokeCurve[1])/
SmokeCurve[2]) + SmokeCurve[0]));
 lcd.print(result);
 lcd.print("ppm     ");
 if(result>1000)
 {
  digitalWrite(buzzer, HIGH);
  delay(2000);
 }
 else
 digitalWrite(buzzer, LOW);
 delay(500);
}
float resistance(int samples, int interval)
{
 int i;
 float res=0;
 for (i=0;i<samples;i++)
 {
  int adc_value=analogRead(sensor);
```

```
        res+=((float)load_Res*(1023-adc_value)/ad-
c_value);
  delay(interval);
 }
 res/=samples;
 return res;
}




float SensorCalibration()
{
 int i;
 float val=0;
 val=resistance(50,500);
 val = val/air_factor;
 return val;
}
```

ANBAZHAGAN K

4. ARDUINO ROBOTIC ARM

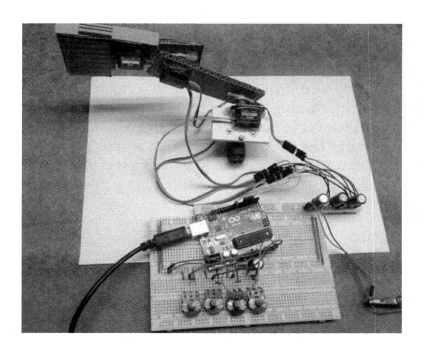

In this instructional exercise, we plan an Arduino Uno Robotic Arm. Whole arm will be planned from some scrap material as well as servos. Whole procedure of development has been clarified in detail underneath. The arm has been worked with cardboards and the individual parts have been bolted to servo engines. Arduino Uno is customized to control servo engines. Servos are filling in as joints of Robotic arm here. This arrangement likewise looks as a Robotic Crane or we can change over it into a Crane by some simple changes. This venture will be exceptionally useful for novices who need to find out how to build up a Simple Robot in minimal effort.

This Arduino Robotic Arm can be constrained by four Potentiometer joined to it, every potentiometer is utilized to control every servo. You can move these servos by turning the pots to pick some object, with some training you can without much of a stretch pick and move the item starting with one spot then onto the next. We have utilized low torque servos here yet you can utilize all the more dominant servos to pick substantial article.

Components Required:

- Arduino Uno

- 100nF Capacitor (four pieces)

- 1000uF Capacitor (four pieces)

- 10K pot-Variable Resistor (four pieces)

- Servo Motor (SG 90-4 pieces)

- Power Supply (5v-ideally 2)

Servo Motor:

First we talk somewhat about Servo Motors. Servo Motors are unreasonably utilized when there is a requirement for precise shaft development or position. These are not proposed for rapid applications. Servo engines are proposed for low speed, medium torque as well as exact position application. So these engines are best for planning mechanical arm.

Servo engines are accessible at various shapes and sizes. We are gonna to utilize little servo engines, here we utilize four SG90 servos. A servo engine will have principally there wires, one is for +ve voltage another is for ground as well as last one is for position setting. The RED wire is associated with control, Black wire is associated with ground and YELLOW wire is associated with signal. Experience this instructional exercise of Controlling Servo Motor utilizing Arduino to become familiar with it. In Arduino we have predefined libraries to control the Servo, so it is extremely simple to control servo, which you will learn alongside this instructional exercise.

Construction of Robotic Arm:

Take a level and stable surface, similar to a table or a hard card board. Next place a servo engine in the center and paste it set up. Ensure the level of revolution is in the region introduced in figure. This servo goes about as base of arm.

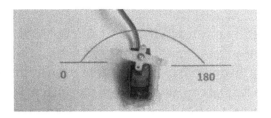

Spot a little bit of cardboard over first servo and afterward place the second servo on this bit of board and paste it set up. The servo pivot must match the graph.

Take a few cardboards and cut them into 3cm x 11cm pieces. Ensure the piece isn't relaxed. Cut a rectangular gap toward one side (leave 0.8cm from base) only enough to fit another servo as well as at another end fit the servo gear firmly with screws or by stick. At that point fit the third servo in the primary opening.

Presently cut another cardboard piece with lengths appeared in figure underneath and stick another rigging at the base of this piece.

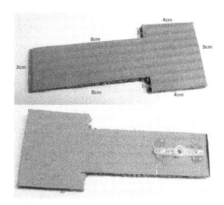

Presently stick the fourth and last servo at the edge of second piece as appeared in figure.

With this, two sorts out resembles.

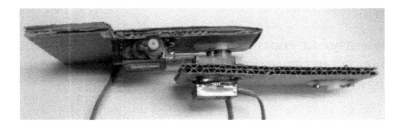

At the point when we append this arrangement to the base it should resemble,

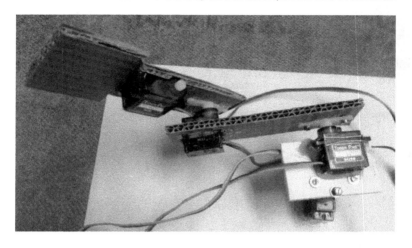

It's nearly done. We simply need to make the snare to get and pick the article like a mechanical hand. For snare, cut another two bits of card leading body of lengths 1cmx7cm and 4cmx5cm. Paste them together as appeared in figure and stick last rigging at the very edge.

Mount this piece on top and with this we have done structure our Robotic Arm.

With this, our essential mechanical arm configuration got finished and that is the means by which we have fabricated our minimal effort automated arm. Presently associate the circuit in breadboard according to circuit outline.

Circuit Diagram and Working Explanation:

The circuit association for Arduino Uno Robotic Arm is demonstrated as follows.

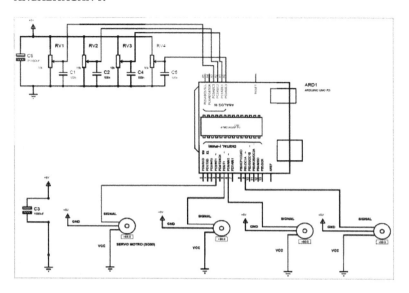

The voltage crosswise over factor resistors isn't totally straight; it will be a boisterous one. So to sift through this clamor, capacitors are put over every resistor as appeared in figure.

Presently we will sustain the voltage gave by these variable resistor (voltage which speaks to position control) into ADC channels of Arduino. We are gonna to utilize four ADC channels of UNO from A0 to A3 for this. After the ADC introduction, we will have computerized estimation of pots speaking to the position required by client. We will take this worth and match it with servo position.

Arduino has six ADC channels. We have utilized four for our Robotic Arm. The UNO ADC is of 10 piece goals so the whole number qualities running from 0-1023 ($2^{\wedge}10 = 1024$ qualities). This implies it will guide input voltages somewhere in the range of 0 as well as 5 volts into number qualities somewhere in the range of 0 and 1023. So for each ($5/1024 = 4.9$mV) per unit. Study mapping the voltage levels utilizing ADC diverts in Arduino here.

Presently, for the UNO to change over simple sign into computerized signal, we have to Use ADC Channel of Arduino Uno, with the assistance of beneath capacities:

1. analogRead(pin);

2. analogReference();

3. analogReadResolution(bits);

Arduino ADC channels have a default reference estimation of 5V. This implies we can give a most extreme information voltage of 5V for ADC transformation at any information channel. Since certain sensors give voltages from 0-2.5V, so with a 5V reference, we get lesser precision, so we have a guidance that empowers us to change this reference esteem. So for changing the reference esteem we have "analogReference();"

As default we get the most extreme board ADC goals

which is 10bits, this goals can be changed by utilizing guidance ("analogReadResolution(bits);").

In our Robotic hand circuit, we have left this reference voltage to the default, so we can peruse an incentive from ADC channel by straightforwardly calling capacity "analogRead(pin);", here "stick" speaks to stick where we associated the simple sign, say we need to peruse "A0". The incentive from ADC can be put away into a number as int SENSORVALUE0 = analogRead(A0);.

Presently how about we talk about the SERVO, the Arduino Uno has a component which empowers us to control the servo situation by simply giving the degree esteem. State in the event that we need the servo to be at 30, we can legitimately speak to the incentive in the program. The SERVO header (Servo.h) record deals with all the obligation proportion computations inside.

```
#include <Servo.h>

servo servo0;

servo0.attach(3);

servo0.write(degrees);
```

Here first explanation speaks to the header document

for controlling the SERVO MOTOR. Second explanation is naming the servo; we leave it as servo0 as we are gonna to utilize four. Third proclamation states where the servo sign stick is associated; this must be a PWM stick. Here we are utilizing PIN3 for first servo. Fourth explanation gives directions for situating servo engine in degrees. On the off chance that it is given 30, the servo engine turns 30 degrees.

Presently, we have SG90 servo situation from 0 to 180 and the ADC esteems are from 0-1023. We will utilize an exceptional capacity which matches the two qualities consequently.

```
sensorvalue0 = map(sensorvalue0, 0, 1023, 0, 180);
```

This announcement maps the two qualities consequently and stores the outcome in whole number 'servovalue0'.

This is the means by which we have controlled the Servos in our Robotic Arm task utilizing Arduino. Check the full code beneath.

How to Operate Robotic Arm:

There are four pots given to the client. Also, by pivoting these four pots, we give variable voltage at the ADC channels of UNO. So the advanced estimations of Arduino are leveled out of client. These advanced qualities are mapped to modify the servo engine position, thus the servo position is responsible for client and by pivoting these Pots client can move the joints of Robotic arm and can pick or snatch any article.

Code

```
#include <Servo.h>
Servo servo0;
Servo servo1;
Servo servo2;
Servo servo3;
int sensorvalue0;
int sensorvalue1;
int sensorvalue2;
int sensorvalue3;
void setup()
{
 pinMode(A0,INPUT);
 pinMode(3,OUTPUT);
 servo0.attach(3);

  pinMode(A1,INPUT);
 pinMode(5,OUTPUT);
 servo1.attach(5);

  pinMode(A2,INPUT);
 pinMode(6,OUTPUT);
 servo2.attach(6);
```

```
  pinMode(A3,INPUT);
  pinMode(9,OUTPUT);
  servo3.attach(9);
}
void loop()
{
  sensorvalue0 = analogRead(A0);
  sensorvalue0 = map(sensorvalue0, 0, 1023, 0, 180);
  servo0.write(sensorvalue0);
  sensorvalue1 = analogRead(A1);
  sensorvalue1 = map(sensorvalue1, 0, 1023, 0, 180);
  servo1.write(sensorvalue1);
  sensorvalue2 = analogRead(A2);
  sensorvalue2 = map(sensorvalue2, 0, 1023, 0, 180);
  servo2.write(sensorvalue2);
  sensorvalue3 = analogRead(A3);
  sensorvalue3 = map(sensorvalue3, 0, 1023, 0, 180);
  servo3.write(sensorvalue3);
}
```

❖ ❖ ❖

5. CELL PHONE CONTROLLED ROBOT CAR UTILIZING G-SENSOR AS WELL AS ARDUINO

We are gonna to Control the Robot Car through the G sensor of our cell phone as well as you will have the option to move the Robot just by flipping the Phone. We will likewise utilize Arduino and RemoteXY application for this G-Sensor Controlled Robot. RemoteXY application is utilized to make the interface in the Smart Phone for controlling the Robot. We will include the joystick in the interface so Robot can be constrained by Joystick just as by tilting the telephone.

G-Sensor or Gravity sensor is essentially Accelerometer in Smart telephone which is utilized to control the screen direction of the telephone. Accelerometer detects the X,Y, Z headings of the Gravitational power and turn the Screen as per arrangement of the Phone. Presently days, increasingly delicate and exact Gyroscope sensor is utilized in mobiles for choosing the direction of the Screen. In our Project, Robot vehicle will move, as per the course wherein telephone is being tilted, similar to when we tilt the telephone forward, at that point vehicle will push ahead and we tilt it down then vehicle will go in reverse. This is same like when we play some vehicle games in Mobile, they additionally use G sensor to move the vehicle as needs be. Check our different Robotics Projects here.

Required Components:

- Two wheel robot car chassis
- Arduino UNO
- L298N Motor Controller
- HC-06 Bluetooth module (HC-05 will work too)
- Power supply or Cells
- Connecting wires

Creating Interface for Robot using RemoteXY app:

For making the interface to control the Robot Car utilizing RemoteXY application, you should go to following connection

http://remotexy.com/en/editorial manager/The site page will resemble this

At that point from the left half of screen, get the switch button and the joystick and spot it in the portable interface. The catch will turn on the light at stick 13 which is associated inside in the Arduino and the joystick will move the robot vehicle. The website page in the wake of putting the switch and the joystick will resemble this.

At that point we should put the empower the G sensor empower/incapacitate button alongside the joystick, with the goal that we can move the Robot Car by tilting the telephone in left, right, here and there course. Utilizing that catch we can empower and cripple G sensor, when G sensor is handicapped Car can be constrained by moving the Joystick. So to put the G sensor empower/impair button, click on the joystick you put in the interface and on the left side there will be a properties area, there will be a choice at last for putting the G sensor catch close to the joystick, so place the G sensor button any place you will like. The website page after this will resemble this.

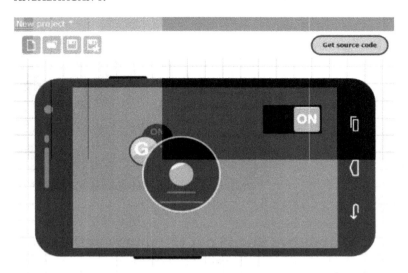

From that point forward, click on the catch "Get source code" and spare it onto your PC. Download the library from here and spare it into the Arduino library envelope. Aggregate the downloaded code to watch that there are no blunders. This isn't the code that will run the Robot yet it will help in utilizing the App with the Arduino. Download the application from here or go to the Play Store as well as install RemoteXY application from that point for you Android Smart Phone.

Circuit Diagram and Explanation:

As a matter of first importance, we will interface the L298N engine controller with the Arduino. Associate the ENA and ENB stick of the engine controller to the

Arduino stick 12 and 11 separately. These two pins are for the PWM control of the engine. Utilizing postulations pins, we can increment or abatement the speed of vehicle. At that point interface the IN1, IN2, IN3 as well as IN4 to the Arduino pins 10, 9, 8 as well as 7 separately. These pins will pivot the engines in the two headings (clockwise and against clockwise).

To control the engine, interface the positive and negative of the battery to the 12V and the ground of the engine controller. At that point associate the 5V and the ground from the engine controller to the Arduino Vin and the ground.

At that point we will associate the Bluetooth module HC-06 with the arduino. In case you have HC-05, at that point it will work as well. Associate the VCC as well as the ground of the Bluetooth module to the 5V as well as the ground of the Arduino. At that point associate the TX stick of Bluetooth Module to the stick 2 of Arduino and the RX stick to the stick 3 of Arduino. Additionally check Bluetooth Controlled Toy Car utilizing Arduino to become familiar with utilizing Bluetooth with Arduino.

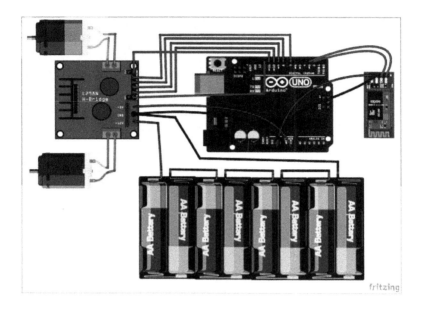

Code Explanation:

Full Arduino code for this Mobile Controlled Robot Car is given underneath in Code area, here we will see how this code is functioning.

Above all else, we have incorporated the libraries for Software Serial and RemoteXY. The RemoteXY library will help us in setting the application with Arduino, through which we will control the robot vehicle. From that point forward, we have characterized the pins for the Bluetooth module, TX from the Bluetooth module is associated with the stick 2 of Arduino which is the RX stick of Arduino and the RX from the Bluetooth module is associated with the stick 3 of the Arduino which is the TX stick of Arduino and set the baud pace of the Bluetooth module at 9600.

```
#define REMOTEXY_MODE__SOFTWARESERIAL

#include <SoftwareSerial.h>        //Including the
software serial library

#include <RemoteXY.h>        //Including the
remotexy library

/* RemoteXY connection settings */

#define REMOTEXY_SERIAL_RX 2        //defining
the pin 2 as RX pin

#define REMOTEXY_SERIAL_TX 3        //defining
the pin 3 as TX pin

#define REMOTEXY_SERIAL_SPEED 9600        //set-
ting baudrate at 9600
```

The accompanying code will increment or reduction the engine speed. At the point when the joystick will be at the inside, the speed will be zero and when it will be the forward way then the speed will increment from zero to 100. The speed will be decline from 0 to - 100 when the vehicle will move in the switch course. The vehicle can likewise be moved explicit speed, this should be possible by giving the PWM signal. The pwm sign will be given to the engines as indicated by the revolution of the joystick.

```
if (motor_speed > 100) motor_speed = 100;

if (motor_speed < -100) motor_speed = -100;

if (motor_speed > 0) {

  digitalWrite(pointer[0], HIGH);

  digitalWrite(pointer[1], LOW);

  analogWrite(pointer[2], motor_speed*2.55);

}

else if (motor_speed < 0) {

  digitalWrite(pointer[0], LOW);

  digitalWrite(pointer[1], HIGH);
```

```
   analogWrite(pointer[2], (-motor_speed)*2.55);

}

else {

   digitalWrite(pointer[0], LOW);

   digitalWrite(pointer[1], LOW);

   analogWrite(pointer[2], 0);

}
```

In the accompanying code, we have characterized the capacity which will be called at whatever point we will move the joystick in the application. At the point when we will turn on the switch in the application then the rationale 1 will be given to the stick 13 of the Arduino which turns On the LED stick. While moving the robot vehicle in the forward and reverse way, the Speed capacity will be called.

```
void loop()

{

   RemoteXY_Handler ();
```

```
digitalWrite (ledpin, (RemoteXY.switch_1==0)?
LOW:HIGH);

Speed (first_motor, RemoteXY.joystick_1_y - Re-
moteXY.joystick_1_x);

Speed (second_motor, RemoteXY.joystick_1_y +
RemoteXY.joystick_1_x);

}
```

How to run it:

Include the library of the RemoteXY to the Arduino libraries and transfer the code in the Arduino IDE. At that point download the application in your cell phone and afterward turn on the Bluetooth. The interface of the application will resemble this

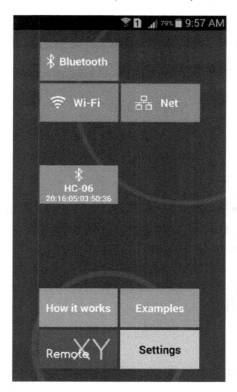

At that point go to Bluetooth and turn on the Bluetooth there. Subsequent to turning it on, it will show you the Bluetooth gadgets. Select your HC-06 Bluetooth module from that point, it will take you to the interface, from where you can control the Robot Car.

This is the means by which we can utilize the Gravity Sensor inside our Mobile telephone to move the Robot. You can further test and discover all the more intriguing utilization of G sensor to control the outside things by interfacing a Microcontorller in the middle of (like Arduino).

Code

```
#define REMOTEXY_MODE__SOFTWARESERIAL
#include <SoftwareSerial.h>      //Including the software serial library
#include <RemoteXY.h>            //Including the remotexy library
/* RemoteXY connection settings */
#define REMOTEXY_SERIAL_RX 2      //defining the pin 2 as RX pin
#define REMOTEXY_SERIAL_TX 3      //defining the pin 3 as TX pin
#define REMOTEXY_SERIAL_SPEED 9600   //setting baudrate at 9600
```

```
unsigned char RemoteXY_CONF[] =          //remotexy
configuration
{ 3,0,23,0,1,5,5,15,41,11
,43,43,1,2,0,6,5,27,11,5
,79,78,0,79,70,70,0 };


struct {                       //Function for declaring the
variables
  signed char joystick_1_x;    //joystick x-axis
  signed char joystick_1_y;    //joystick y-axis
  unsigned char switch_1;      //variables for switch
  unsigned char connect_flag;
} RemoteXY;
//defining the pins for first motor
#define IN1 10
#define IN2 9
#define ENA 12
//defining the pins for second motor
#define IN3 8
#define IN4 7
#define ENB 11
//defining the LED pin
#define ledpin 13
unsigned char first_motor[3] =
{IN1, IN2, ENA};
unsigned char second_motor[3] =
{IN3, IN4, ENB};
void Speed (unsigned char * pointer, int motor_speed)
{
```

```
if(motor_speed>100) motor_speed=100;
if(motor_speed<-100) motor_speed=-100;
if(motor_speed>0) {
 digitalWrite(pointer[0], HIGH);
 digitalWrite(pointer[1], LOW);
 analogWrite(pointer[2], motor_speed*2.55);
}
else if(motor_speed<0) {
 digitalWrite(pointer[0], LOW);
 digitalWrite(pointer[1], HIGH);
 analogWrite(pointer[2], (-motor_speed)*2.55);
}
else {
 digitalWrite(pointer[0], LOW);
 digitalWrite(pointer[1], LOW);
 analogWrite(pointer[2], 0);
}
}
void setup()
{
 //defining the motor pins as the output pins
 pinMode (IN1, OUTPUT);
 pinMode (IN2, OUTPUT);
 pinMode (IN3, OUTPUT);
 pinMode (IN4, OUTPUT);
 pinMode (ledpin, OUTPUT);
 RemoteXY_Init ();
}
void loop()
{
```

```
RemoteXY_Handler ();
  digitalWrite (ledpin, (RemoteXY.switch_1==0)?
LOW:HIGH);
  Speed (first_motor, RemoteXY.joystick_1_y - RemoteXY.joystick_1_x);
  Speed (second_motor, RemoteXY.joystick_1_y + RemoteXY.joystick_1_x);
}
```

◆ ◆ ◆

6. ARDUINO BASED AUTOMATIC PLANT IRRIGATION SYSTEM WITH MESSAGE ALERT

At whatever point we leave town for hardly any days, we constantly used to stress over our plants as they need water on customary premise. Here we are making programmed plant water system framework using Arduino, which naturally offers water to your plants as well as keep you invigorated by sending message to your mobile phone.

This plant watering framework soil dampness sensor checks the sogginess level in the earth as well as on the off chance that sogginess level is low, at that point Arduino turns On a water siphon to give water to the plant. Water siphon gets consequently off when framework discovers enough dampness in the dirt. At whatever point framework turned On or off the siphon, a message is sent to the client by means of Global System for Mobile module, refreshing the status of water siphon and soil dampness. This framework is extremely helpful in Farms, gardens, home as well as so on. This structure is completely automated as well as there is no necessity for any human intervention.

Required Components for Arduino Plant Watering System Project

- Arduino Uno
- Transistor BC547 (2)
- GSM Module
- 16x2 LCD (optional)
- Connecting wires
- Relay 12v
- Power supply 12v 1A
- Soil Moisture Sensor
- Water cooler pump
- Variable Resister (10k, 100k)
- Resistors (1k, 10k)
- Voltage Regulator IC LM317

- Terminal connector

Global System for Mobile Module:

We have used TTL SIM800 Global System for Mobile module. The SIM800 is a finished Quad-band Global System for Mobile/General Packet Radio Service Module which can be inserted effectively by client or specialist. SIM900 Global System for Mobile Module gives an industry-standard interface; the SIM800 conveys Global System for Mobile/General Packet Radio Service 850/900/1800/1900MHz execution for voice, SMS, Data with low power usage. The plan of this SIM800 Global System for Mobile Module is thin as well as conservative. It is effectively accessible in the market or online from eBay.

- Quad - band Global System for Mobile/General Packet Radio Service module in little size.

- GPRS Enabled

- TTL Output

Become familiar with GSM module and AT directions here. Likewise check our different ventures utilizing GSM and Arduino for appropriately comprehend their interfacing.

Circuit Explanation:

In this plant water system framework , we have utilized a natively constructed soil dampness sensor test to detect the dirt dampness level. To make test, we have cut and carved a Copper clad Board as per the

Picture demonstrated as follows. One side of the test is legitimately associated with Vcc and other test terminal goes to the base of BC547 transistor. A potentiometer is associated with the base of the transistor to alter the affectability of the sensor.

Arduino is utilized for controlling entire the procedure of this Automatic Plant Watering System. The yield of soil sensor circuit is straightforwardly associated with advanced stick D7 of Arduino. A LED is utilized at the sensor circuit, this current LED's ON state shows the nearness of dampness in the dirt and OFF state demonstrates the absense of dampness in the dirt.

GSM module is utilized for sending SMS to the client. Here we have utilized TTL SIM800 GSM module, which gives and takes TTL rationale legitimately (client may utilize any GSM module). A LM317 Voltage controller is utilized to control the SIM800 GSM module. LM317 is touchy to voltage rating and it is prescribed to peruse its datasheet before use. Its working voltage rating is 3.8v to 4.2v (if it's not too much trouble lean toward 3.8v to work it). The following is the Circuit Diagram of Power Supply given to the TTL sim800 GSM Module:

On the off chance that client needs to utilize SIM900 TTL Module, at that point he should utilize 5V and on the off chance that the client needs to utilize SIM900 Module, at that point apply 12v in the DC Jack space of the board.

A 12V Relay is used to control the 220VAC little water siphon. The hand-off is driven by a BC547 Transistor which is additionally associated with computerized stick 11 of Arduino.

A discretionary LCD is likewise utilized for showing status and messages. Control pins of LCD, RS and EN are associated with stick 14 and 15 of Arduino and information pins of LCD D4-D7 are straightforwardly associated at stick 16, 17, 18 and 19 of Arduino. LCD is utilized in 4-piece mode and driven by Arduino's inbuilt LCD library.

The following is the circuit graph of this Irrigation System with arduino and soil dampness sensor:

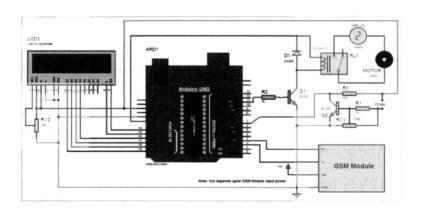

Working Explanation:

Working of this Automatic Plant Irrigation System is very basic. As a matter of first importance, it is a Completely Automated System and there is no need of labor to control the framework. Arduino is utilized for controlling the entire procedure and GSM module is utilized for sending ready messages to client on his Cellphone.

In case dampness is available in soil, at that point there is conduction among the 2 tests of Soil Moisture sensor and because of this conduction, transistor Q2 stays in activated/on state as well as Arduino Pin D7 stays Low. When Arduino peruses LOW sign at D7, at that point it sends SMS to client about "Soil Moisture is Normal. Engine killed" and water siphon stays in Off state.

Presently on the off chance that there is no Moisture in soil, at that point Transistor Q2 gets Off and Pin D7 turns out to be High. At that point Arduino peruses the Pin D7 and turns On the water engine and furthermore sends message to client about "Low Soil Moisture distinguished. Engine turned ON". Engine will consequently mood killer when there is adequate dampness in the dirt. Further check the Code (given toward the end) for better understanding the task working process.

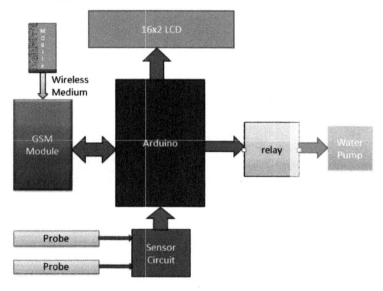

Programming Explanation:

Code for this program is effectively justifiable. As a matter of first importance we have included SoftwareSerial library to make stick 2 and 3 as Rx and Tx and furthermore included LiquidCrystal for LCD. At that point we characterized a few factors for engine, soil dampness sensor, LED and so on.

```
#include<SoftwareSerial.h>

SoftwareSerial Serial1(2,3);

#include<LiquidCrystal.h>

LiquidCrystal lcd(14,15,16,17,18,19);

int led=13;

int flag=0;

String str="";

#define motor 11

#define sensor 7
```

At that point in void arrangement () work, sequential correspondence is introduced at 9600 bps and bearings are given to the different Pins. gsmInit capacity is called for instate the GSM module.

```
Serial1.begin(9600);

Serial.begin(9600);

pinMode(led, OUTPUT);

pinMode(motor, OUTPUT);

pinMode(sensor, INPUT_PULLUP);

lcd.print("Water Irrigaton");

lcd.setCursor(4,1);

delay(2000);

lcd.clear();

lcd.print("Hello world");

lcd.setCursor(0,1);

lcd.print("Welcomes You");

delay(2000);

gsmInit();
```

At that point sensor is perused in void circle () capacity, and engine is turned on or off as per the sensor status and a SMS is likewise being sent to the client utilizing sendSMS work. Check the different capacities in full code given toward the end.

```
void loop()

{

  lcd.setCursor(0,0);

  lcd.print("Automatic Mode   ");

  if(digitalRead(sensor)==1 && flag==0)

  {

    delay(1000);

    if(digitalRead(sensor)==1)

    {

    digitalWrite(led, HIGH);

    sendSMS("Low Soil Moisture detected. Motor turned ON");
```

```
lcd.begin(16,2);

lcd.setCursor(0,1);

...........

.........
```

Here the gsmInit () capacity is significant and clients for the most part think that its hard to set assuming appropriately. It is utilized to introduce the GSM module, where initially GSM module is checked whether it is associated or not by sending 'AT' direction to GSM module. In the event that reaction OK is gotten, implies it is prepared. Framework continues checking for the module until it gets prepared or until 'alright' is gotten. At that point ECHO is killed by sending the ATE0 order, generally GSM module will reverberate every one of the directions. At that point at long last Network accessibility is checked through the 'AT+CPIN?' order, whenever embedded card is SIM card and PIN is available, it gives the reaction READY. This is additionally check over and over until the system is found.

```
void gsmInit()

{
```

```
lcd.clear();

lcd.print("Finding Module..");

boolean at_flag=1;

while(at_flag)

{

  Serial1.println("AT");

  while(Serial1.available()>0)

  {

    if(Serial1.find("OK"))

      at_flag=0;

  }

  delay(1000);

}
```

....

....

So with this Automatic Irrigation System, you don't have to stress over your plants when you are away from your home. It very well may be additionally upgraded to be worked and checked over the web.

Code

```
#include<SoftwareSerial.h>
SoftwareSerial Serial1(2,3);
#include<LiquidCrystal.h>
LiquidCrystal lcd(14,15,16,17,18,19);
int led=13;
int flag=0;
String str="";
#define motor 11
#define sensor 7
void setup()
{
 lcd.begin(16,2);
 Serial1.begin(9600);
 Serial.begin(9600);
 pinMode(led, OUTPUT);
 pinMode(motor, OUTPUT);
 pinMode(sensor, INPUT_PULLUP);
 lcd.print("Water Irrigaton");
 lcd.setCursor(4,1);
 delay(2000);
 lcd.clear();
 lcd.print("Hello world");
 lcd.setCursor(0,1);
 lcd.print("Welcomes You");
```

```
delay(2000);
gsmInit();
lcd.clear();
lcd.print("System Ready");
}
void loop()
{
  lcd.setCursor(0,0);
  lcd.print("Automatic Mode  ");
  if(digitalRead(sensor)==1 && flag==0)
  {
   delay(1000);
   if(digitalRead(sensor)==1)
   {
    digitalWrite(led, HIGH);
        sendSMS("Low Soil Moisture detected. Motor
turned ON");
    lcd.begin(16,2);
    lcd.setCursor(0,1);
    lcd.print("Motor ON  ");
    digitalWrite(motor, HIGH);
    delay(2000);
    flag=1;
   }
  }
  else if(digitalRead(sensor)==0 && flag==1)
  {
   delay(1000);
   if(digitalRead(sensor)==0)
   {
```

```
    digitalWrite(led, LOW);
    sendSMS("Soil Moisture is Normal. Motor turned
OFF");
    digitalWrite(motor, LOW);
    lcd.begin(16,2);
    lcd.print("Motor OFF");
    lcd.setCursor(0,1);
    lcd.print("Motor OFF");
    delay(2000);
    flag=0;
  }
 }
}


void sendSMS(String msg)
{
 lcd.clear();
 lcd.print("Sending SMS");
 Serial1.println("AT+CMGF=1");
 delay(500);
 Serial1.print("AT+CMGS=");
 Serial1.print("");
 Serial1.print("+919610126059");  // number
 Serial1.print("");
 Serial1.println();
 delay(500);
 Serial1.println(msg);
 delay(500);
 Serial1.write(26);
 delay(1000);
```

```
lcd.clear();
lcd.print("SMS Sent");
delay(1000);
lcd.begin(16,2);
}
void gsmInit()
{
lcd.clear();
lcd.print("Finding Module..");
boolean at_flag=1;
while(at_flag)
{
 Serial1.println("AT");
 while(Serial1.available()>0)
 {
  if(Serial1.find("OK"))
  at_flag=0;
 }
 delay(1000);
}
Serial1.println("ATE0");
lcd.clear();
lcd.print("Finding Network..");
boolean net_flag=1;
while(net_flag)
{
 Serial1.println("AT+CPIN?");
 while(Serial1.available()>0)
 {
  if(Serial1.find("READY"))
```

```
    net_flag=0;
    break;
  }
  delay(1000);
}
Serial1.println("AT+CNMI=2,2,0,0,0");
delay(1000);
Serial1.println("AT+CMGF=1");
delay(1000);
Serial1.println("AT+CSMP=17,167,0,0");
lcd.clear();
Serial1.flush();
}
```

❖ ❖ ❖

7. LOOKING OVER TEXT DISPLAY ON 8X8 LED MATRIX UTILIZING ARDUINO

In this instructional exercise we are gonna to structure a 8x8 LED Matrix Scrolling Display utilizing Arduino Uno, which will show looking over letter sets.

8x8 LED Matrix contains 64 LEDs (Light Emitting Diodes) which are masterminded as a grid, subse-

ANBAZHAGAN K

quently the name is LED lattice. We are gonna to make this Matrix by welding these 64 LEDs on to the perfboard or DOT PCB. The LEDs can be of any shading, pick the ones which are accessible with you. At that point we will compose a program for Arduino to control these 64 LEDs lattice. The UNO, as per program, powers proper LEDs to show characters in looking over design.

Components Required:

- Arduino Uno
- Perfboard with other binding devices
- 64 LEDs
- Power Supply (5v)
- 1K? resistor (Eight pieces)

Circuit and Working Explanation:

There are 64 LEDs masterminded in a grid structure. So we have 8 sections and 8 lines. Over those lines and segments, all the positive terminals straight are united. For each line, there is one Common Positive Terminal for every one of the 8 LED in that line. It is appeared in beneath figure,

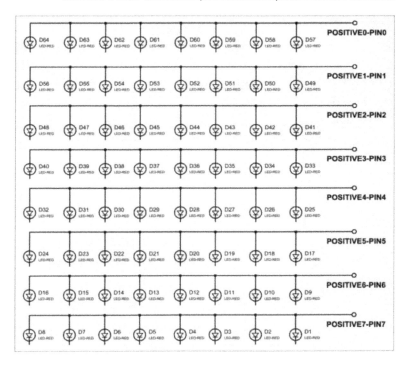

So for 8 lines we have 8 regular positive terminals. Think about the main column, as found in the figure, 8 LEDs from D57 to D64 have a typical positive terminal and are meant by 'POSITIVE0'. Presently in the event that we need shine one or all LEDs in the main ROW of grid, at that point we should control the PIN0 of LED Matrix. Moreover in the event that we need to shine any LED (or all) in any ROW then we have to control the relating Common Positive Terminal Pin of that separate Row.

This isn't finished at this point and simply leaving the

MATRIX ROWS with positive stockpile won't yield anything. We have to ground the LEDs -ves to sparkle them. So in 8x8 LED grid, all the negative terminals of the LEDs in any segment are united to frame eight Common Negative Terminals, similar to all the negative terminals in first section are associated together to the PIN-A1 (NEGATIVE7). This is appeared in beneath figure:

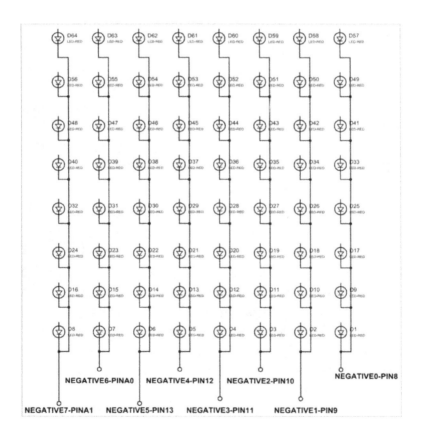

One should focus on these pins while fastening the LEDs on Perfboard.

Presently in the event that we have to ground any LED in the primary section, at that point we will ground the PIN-A1 (NEGATIVE7) of the MATRIX, and it will ground every one of the LEDs in first segment. A similar procedure goes for the various seven regular negative sections.

Since now you realize how Common Positive and Common Negative functions. How about we set up them together to perceive how they cooperate and the last Circuit for Scrolling 8x8 LED Matrix show will resemble this:

z

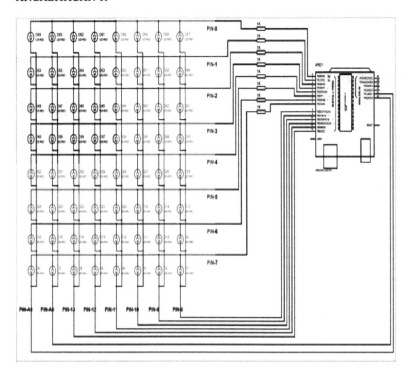

Driving 8x8 LED Matrix utilizing Multiplexing:

Presently suppose we need to turn ON LED57 then we have to control PIN0 of UNO and ground the PIN-8 of UNO. Presently for turning both LED57 as well as LED50 on, we have to control PIN0, PIN1 as well as ground the PIN8, PIN9. In any case, doing so won't just turn on D57, D50 yet in addition D49, D58. To stay away from that we utilize a method called Multiplexing. We have just examined this Multiplex Technique in 8x8 LED Matrix in detail; experience that article for itemized clarification. Here we are clarifying the

Multiplexing quickly.

The human eye can't catch a recurrence in excess of 30 HZ. That is if a LED goes ON and OFF consistently at the pace of 30HZ or more. The eye considers the To be as persistently ON. Anyway this isn't the situation and LED will be really turning ON as well as OFF continually. This method is called Multiplexing.

Suppose for instance, we need to just turn on LED57 and LED50 without turning on D49 and D58. Stunt is, we will initially give capacity to initially column to turn ON LED57 and hang tight for 1mSEC, and afterward we will turn it OFF. At that point we will give capacity to second column to turn on LED50 and hang tight for 1mSEC at that point will turn it OFF. The cycle goes consistently with high recurrence and LED57 and LED50 will jumping On and Off quickly and both the LEDs will give off an impression of being persistently ON to our eye. Means we are just giving capacity to the each line in turn, taking out the odds of turning on different LEDs in different lines. We will utilize this system to show all characters.

There is additionally a library called LedControlMS.h to take care the entirety of this multifaceted nature of multiplexing, where you just need to enter the character or number which you need to print on LED lattice, check this Arduino LED grid with MAX7219 venture for more detail.

Programming Explanation:

In our Code, we have composed decimal incentive for each character and customized these qualities into the Arduino. The program has written to move these qualities to next line for each 0.2 sec, this will be viewed as looking of characters upwards, it's extremely basic.

To change the characters to be shown, simply supplant the incentive in the scorch ALPHA[] cluster as per the character esteems given underneath,

24,60,102,126,102,102,102,0,0,0,   // A

124,102,102,124,102,102,124,0,0,0,   // B

60,102,96,96,96,102,60,0, 0,0,   // C

120,108,102,102,102,108,120,0, 0,0,   // D

126,96,96,120,96,96,126,0, 0,0,   // E

126,96,96,120,96,96,96,0, 0,0,   // F

60,102,96,110,102,102,60,0, 0,0,   // G

102,102,102,126,102,102,102,0, 0,0,   // H

60,24,24,24,24,24,60,0, 0,0,   // I

```
30,12,12,12,12,108,56,0, 0,0,              // J

102,108,120,112,120,108,102,0, 0,0,        // K

96,96,96,96,96,96,126,0, 0,0,              // L

99,119,127,107,99,99,99,0, 0,0,            // M

102,118,126,126,110,102,102,0, 0,0,        // N

60,102,102,102,102,102,60,0, 0,0,          // O

124,102,102,124,96,96,96,0, 0,0,           // P

60,102,102,102,102,60,14,0, 0,0,           // Q

124,102,102,124,120,108,102,0, 0,0,        // R

60,102,96,60,6,102,60,0, 0,0,              // S

126,24,24,24,24,24,24,0, 0,0,              // T

102,102,102,102,102,102,60,0, 0,0,         // U

102,102,102,102,102,60,24,0, 0,0,          // V

99,99,99,107,127,119,99,0, 0,0,            // W

102,102,60,24,60,102,102,0, 0,0,           // X
```

102,102,102,60,24,24,24,0,0,0,   // Y

126,6,12,24,48,96,126,0,0,0,   // Z

Like in the event that you need to show DAD on the LED Matrix, at that point initially supplant the Characters esteems in the roast ALPHA[] exhibit by putting esteems for characters D,A and D from the above rundown:

char ALPHA[] = {0,0,0,0,0,0,0,0,0,0,0,

120,108,102,102,102,108,120,0,0,0,

24,60,102,126,102,102,102,0,0,0,

120,108,102,102,102,108,120,0,0,0,

0,0,0,0,0,0,0,0,0,0,0};

Complete esteems are currently 5*10=50 qualities, so

Replace,

for(int x=0;x<142;x++) //150-8(to stop overflow)

{........

With,

```
for(int x=0;x<42;x++) //50-8(to stop overflow)
{........
```

So you simply need to change the number.

With this you have done the programming and now you can look over any content on the 8x8 LED Matrix, check the Full code beneath.

Code

```
char ground[8] = {8,9,10,11,12,13,A0,A1};
char ALPHA[] = {0,0,0,0,0,0,0,0,0,0,0,
60,102,96,96,96,102,60,0,0,0,
60,24,24,24,24,24,60,0,0,0,
124,102,102,124,120,108,102,0,0,0,
60,102,96,96,96,102,60,0,0,0,
102,102,102,102,102,102,60,0,0,0,
60,24,24,24,24,24,60,0,0,0,
126,24,24,24,24,24,24,0,0,0,
120,108,102,102,102,108,120,0,0,0,
60,24,24,24,24,24,60,0,0,0,
60,102,96,110,102,102,60,0,0,0,
126,96,96,120,96,96,126,0,0,0,
60,102,96,60,6,102,60,0,0,0,
126,24,24,24,24,24,24,0,0,0,
0,0,0,0,0,0,0,0,0,0,0
};
```

```
void setup()
{
 for (int x=8;x<14;x++)
 {
  pinMode(x, OUTPUT);
 }
 pinMode(A0, OUTPUT);
 pinMode(A1, OUTPUT);

  for (int i=0;i<8;i++)
 {
  digitalWrite(ground[i],HIGH);
 }
 DDRD = 0xFF;
 PORTD =0;
}
void loop()
{
 for(int x=0;x<142;x++)
 {
  for(int a=0;a<20;a++)
  {
    for (int i=0;i<8;i++)
    {
     digitalWrite(ground[i],LOW);
     PORTD = ALPHA[i+x];
     delay(1);
     digitalWrite(ground[i],HIGH);
    }
  }
 }
```

```
}
delay(1000);
}
```

❖ ❖ ❖

8. 12V BATTERY CHARGER CIRCUIT UTILIZING LM317 (12V POWER SUPPLY)

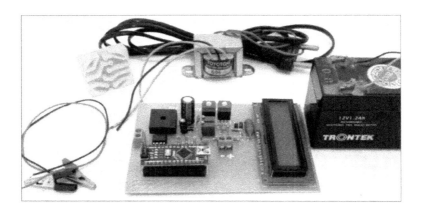

The vast majority of our gadgets tasks are controlled by a Lead Acid battery, in this venture let us talk about how to energize this lead corrosive Battery with an assistance of a straightforward circuit that can be effectively comprehended and worked from home. This venture will spare yourself from putting resources into a battery charger and help you to broaden your battery life. So we should get started!!!!

We should begin by understanding barely any essential things about a Lead Acid Battery with the goal that we can construct our charger all the more proficiently. The greater part of the lead corrosive batteries in the market are 12V batteries. The Ah (Ampere hours) of every battery may fluctuate dependent on the necessary limit, a 7 Ah battery for instance will have the option to give 1 Amps to a term of 7 hours (1 Amps *7 hours = 7 Ah). Presently after complete release the battery rate ought to be around 10.5, this is the ideal opportunity for us to charge our batteries. The charging current of a battery is prescribed to be 1/tenth of the Ah rating of the battery. So for a 7 Ah battery the charging current ought to be around 0.7 Amps. Current more prominent than this may hurt the battery bringing about decreased battery life. Keeping this in thought this, little custom made charger will have the option to give you variable voltage and variable current. The current can be balanced dependent on the present Ah rating of the battery.

This Lead Acid Battery charger circuit can likewise be utilized to charge your cell phones, in the wake of altering the voltage and current as indicated by cell phone, utilizing the POT. This circuit will give a Regulated DC Power Supply from the AC mains and will function as AC-DC Adapter; I have recently made a Variable Power Supply with High present and voltage yield.

Components Required:

- Transformer 12V 1Amp
- IC LM317 (2)

- Diode Bridge W005
- Connector Terminal Block (2)
- Capacitor 1000uF, 1uF
- Capacitor 0.1uF (5)
- Resistor 1k (5)
- Variable resistor 100R
- Diode- Nn007 (3)
- Resistor 10k
- 0.05R - Shunt Resistor/wire
- LM358 - Opamp
- Arduino Nano (optional)
- LCD-16*2 (optional)

Circuit Explanation:

The total schematics of this Battery Charger Circuit are demonstrated as follows:

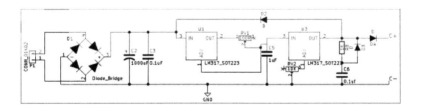

The principle goal of our 12V power supply circuit is to control the voltage as well as current for the battery with the goal that it tends to be charged in the most ideal manner. For this reason we have utilized two LM317 ICs, one is utilized to control the voltage and the other is utilized to restrict the current. Here, in our circuit the IC U1 is utilized to control the current and the IC U3 is utilized to control the voltage. I would firmly prescribe you to peruse the datasheet of LM317 and get it, so it proves to be useful while attempting comparative undertakings since LM317 is a most utilized Variable controller.

Voltage Regulator Circuit:

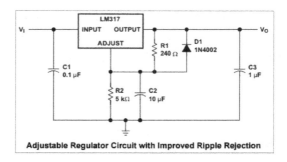

Adjustable Regulator Circuit with Improved Ripple Rejection

A basic Voltage Regulator Circuit, taken from LM317's datasheet, is appeared in the figure above. Here the yield voltage is chosen by the resistor esteems R1 and R2, for our situation the resistor R2 is utilized as a variable resistor to control the yield voltage. The formulae to figure the yield voltage is Vout = 1.25 (1+R2/R1). Utilizing this formulae, the estimation of obstruction 1K (R8) and 10K – pot (RV2) is chosen. You can likewise utilize this LM317 number cruncher to ascertain the estimation of R2.

Current Limiter Circuit:

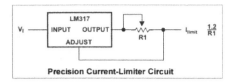

Precision Current-Limiter Circuit

The Current Limiter Circuit, taken from LM317's datasheet, is appeared in the above figure; this is a basic circuit which can be utilized to restrict the current in our circuit dependent on the opposition esteem R1. The formulae to ascertain the yield current is Iout= 1.2/R1. In light of these formulae the estimation of pot RV1 is chosen as 100R.

Subsequently, so as to control the current as well as voltage two potentiometers RV1 as well as RV2 are utilized individually as appeared in the schematics above. The LM317 is controlled by a diode connect; the Diode Bridge itself is associated with a Transformer through connector P1. The rating of the transformer is 12V 1 Amps. This circuit alone is adequate for us to make a straightforward circuit, yet with assistance of hardly any extra set up we can screen the current and voltage of our charger on LCD, which is clarified beneath.

Display Voltage and Current on LCD using Arduino:

With the assistance of an Arduino Nano and a LCD (16*2), we can show the voltage and current estimations of our charger. In any case, how might we do this!!

Arduino Nano is 5V operational Microcontroller, anything over 5V will slaughter it. Be that as it may, our charger chips away at 12V, consequently with the assistance of a Voltage divider circuit the estimation of (0-14) Volt is mapped down to (0-5)V utilizing resistor R1 (1k) and R2 (500R), like have recently done in 0-24v 3A Regulated Power Supply Circuit, to show the Voltage on LCD utilizing Arduino Nano.

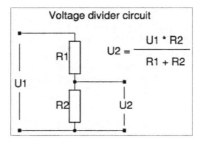

To quantify the present we utilize a shunt resistor R4 of low an incentive to make a voltage drop over the resistor, as should be obvious in the circuit beneath. Presently utilizing Ohms Law mini-computer we can figure the present going through the resistor utilizing the formulae I=V/R.

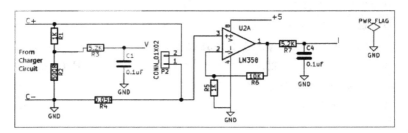

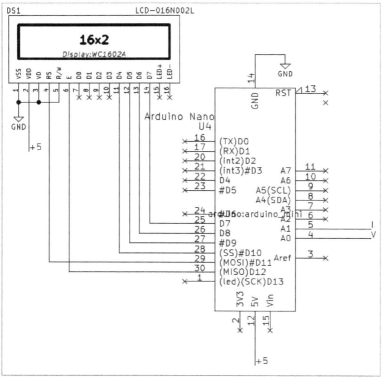

In our circuit the estimation of R4 is 0.05R and the greatest current that can go through our circuit will be 1.2 Amps in light of the fact that the transformer is appraised so. The power rating of the resistor can be determined utilizing $P=I^2 R$. For our situation $P=(1.2*1.2*0.05) => 0.07$ which is not exactly a quarter watt. In any case, in the event that you don't get a 0.05R or in case your present rating is higher, at that point compute the Power in like manner. Presently on the off chance that we can quantify the voltage drop over the resistor R4, we would have the option to compute the current through the circuit utilizing our Arduino. Be that as it may, this voltage drop is negligible for our Arduino to understand it. Thus an Amplifier circuit is built utilizing Op-amp LM358 as appeared in the figure over, the yield of this Op-Amp is given to our Arduino through a R-C circuit to gauge the current and show in on the LCD.

When we choose our estimation of parts in our circuit, it is constantly prescribed to utilize reenactment programming to confirm our qualities before we continue with our real equipment. Here, I have utilized Proteus 8 to reproduce the circuit as demonstrated as follows. You can run the reproduction utilizing the document (12V_charger.pdsprj) given in this compress record.

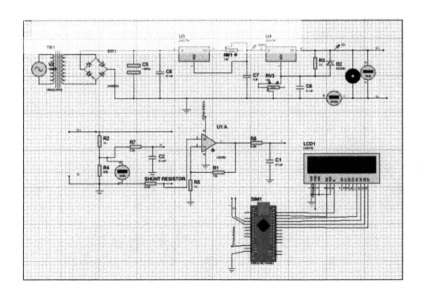

Building up the Battery Charger:

When you are prepared with the circuit you can fire working up your charger, you can either utilize a Perfboard for this undertaking or assemble your own PCB. I have utilized a PCB, the PCB was made utilizing KICAD. KICAD is open source PCB planning programming and can be downloaded online for nothing. In case you are inexperienced with PCB planning, no worries!!!. I have joined the Gerber and other print documents (download here), which can be given over to your nearby PCB producer and your board can be manufactured. You can likewise perceive how your PCB will care for assembling, by transferring these Gerber documents (compress record) to any Gerber Viewer. The PCB structure of our charger is demonstrated as follows.

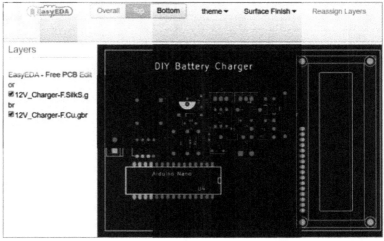

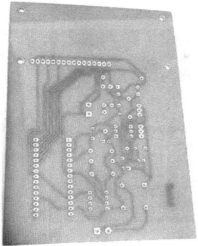

When the PCB is manufactured, gather and bind the segments dependent on qualities given in the schematics, for your benefit a BOM (Bill of materials) is likewise connected in the compress document given above, with the goal that you can buy and amass them calm. Subsequent to amassing our Charger should look something like this....

Testing of Battery Charger:

Presently the time has come to test our charger, the Arduino and LCD isn't required for the charger to work. They are utilized distinctly for observing reason. You can mount them utilizing Bergstick as appeared above, with the goal that you can evacuate them when you need them for another venture.

For testing reason evacuate the Arduino and interface your transformer, presently alter the yield voltage to our necessary voltage utilizing the POT RV2. Confirm the voltage utilizing a multimeter and interface it to the battery as demonstrated as follows. That is it our charger is currently operational.

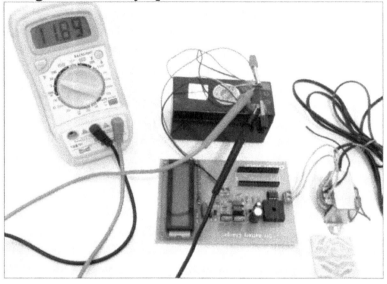

Presently before we plug in our Arduino test the approaching voltage to our Arduino Nano stick A0 and A1, it ought not surpass 5V if out circuit is working appropriately. In the event that all is well associate your Arduino and LCD. Utilize the given underneath Program to transfer in your Arduino. This program will simply show the Voltage and Current estimation of our charger, we can utilize this to set our voltage and screen if our battery is being charged accurately.

In the event that everything fills in true to form, you ought to get a presentation on LCD as appeared in the past figures. Presently, everything is done, we should simply interface our charger to any 12V battery and charge it utilizing a favored voltage and current. Same charger can likewise be utilized to charge your cell phone, however check the current and voltage rating expected to charge the cell phone, before interfacing. You likewise need to connect USB link to our circuit to charge mobile phone.

Upbeat LEARNING!!!!

Code

```
#include <LiquidCrystal.h>
// initialize the library with the numbers of the interface pins
LiquidCrystal lcd(11, 12, 10, 9, 8, 7);
float voltage,current;
void setup()
{
 Serial.begin(9600);
 // set up the LCD's number of columns and rows:
 lcd.begin(16, 2);
 // Print a message to the LCD.
 lcd.setCursor(0, 0);
 lcd.print("12V Charger");
 lcd.setCursor(0, 1);
```

```
lcd.print("-Hello World");
delay(2000);
lcd.clear();
lcd.setCursor(0, 0);
lcd.print("Voltage = ");
lcd.setCursor(0, 1);
lcd.print("Current = ");
}
void loop()
{
 voltage = (analogRead(A0)) * 0.0140625;
 current = (analogRead(A1)) * 0.35;


 lcd.setCursor(10,0);
lcd.print(voltage);
lcd.setCursor(10,1);
lcd.print(current);


 delay(1000);
}
```

❖ ❖ ❖

9. ARDUINO PROPELLER DROVE SHOW

you have seen propellers in air ships or in marine boats, in the event that not in genuine, at that point in motion pictures without a doubt. We are gonna to plan a Propeller Display with Arduino, LEDs as well as a DC engine. In this Propeller Display, content will seem, by all accounts, to be turning in propeller design in a round shape.

The propeller show is in a manner like LED Matrix. It contains 8 LEDs which are orchestrated as a 8*1 network (8 lines and 1 section). They are organized as stepping stool one over the other. These 8 LED can be made to show any substance like content, numbers, images and so on. This is accomplished by Perception of Vision (POV), in which many still pictures are moved rapidly individually in a succession, which gives an impression of liveliness or a moving picture. How this is done is clarified in the instructional exercise given underneath.

Components Required:

- DC Motor
- Arduino Uno
- LED (8 pieces)
- +3.6V LI-ION battery
- 1K? resistor (8 pieces)

Construction of Propeller Display:

First take a steady base; I utilized an old PC DVD DRIVE which was lying near. You can get a wooden board or a cardboard box. At that point make an opening in DVD Drive (base) and supplement the DC engine pivot in it. Ensure the gap is tight enough to hold the engine and engine can turn unreservedly. I utilized Feviquick to set up the hub.

Bolster the highest point of Motor to liken the uneven knocks. I utilized a speck board over it and utilized brisk paste again to leave it with DC engine.

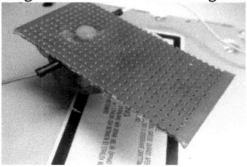

Join the LI-ION battery on top. In the event that

you don't have LI-ION battery of same size, simply leave it. After that step through each LED and examination it with button cell or some other source. At that point take a few resistors and patch them with LEDs according to the image and circuit graph demonstrated as follows.

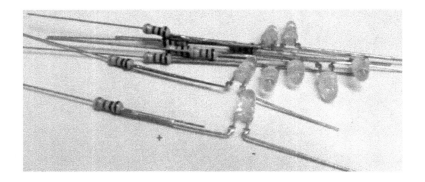

Interface the bound LEDs and resistors with Arduino UNO as appeared in beneath figure and circuit outline.

Mount the UNO on to the highest point of DC MOTOR and secure it with the assistance of cello tape to complete the arrangement. So the last Propeller arrangement will look like beneath:

Circuit and Working Explanation:

Circuit of Arduino controlled POV Display is exceptionally basic, we basically associated 8 LEDs with Arduino Uno according to circuit outline underneath.

PORTD, PIN0 - - LED8 POSITIVE TERMINAL

PORTD, PIN1 - - LED7 POSITIVE TERMINAL

PORTD, PIN2 - - LED6 POSITIVE TERMINAL

PORTD, PIN3 - - LED5 POSITIVE TERMINAL

PORTD, PIN4 - - LED4 POSITIVE TERMINAL

PORTD, PIN5 - - LED3 POSITIVE TERMINAL

PORTD, PIN6 - - LED2 POSITIVE TERMINAL

PORTD, PIN7 - - LED1 POSITIVE TERMINAL

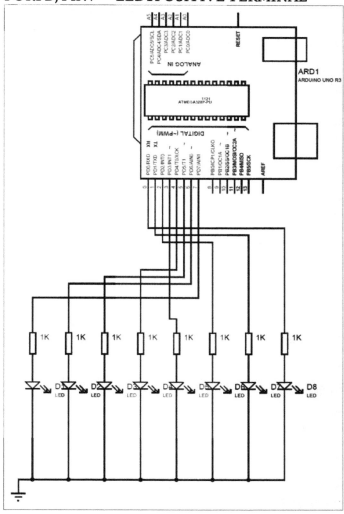

Like we include more sections in 8x8 LED Matrix to broaden the presentation, similarly as opposed to including more LED COLUMNS we move the principal LED COLUMN to the second LED COLUMN place by utilizing the movement of DC MOTOR.

So as to comprehend the entire circumstance, state we need 'A' to be shown by the propeller show. Consider the LED 'needle' is at POSITION1 from the start as appeared in figure beneath. Driven Needle is the Column of eight LEDs.

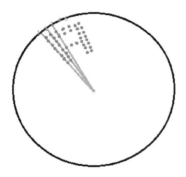

Presently we self control the engine and it will begin running.

At t=0ms: the needle will be at POSITION 1. At this position all the eight leds from top drove msb to base drove lsb ,are fueled on.

At t=1ms: the needle will be at POSITION 2. Same as Position one, at this position all the 8 LEDs, from TOP

LED (MSB) to BOTTOM LED (LSB), are controlled on.

At t = 2ms: the needle will be at POSITION 3. At this position just LED7, LED6 and LED3 remain ON as well as remaining LEDs are killed.

At t = 3ms: the needle will be at POSITION 4. Same as Position three, at this position just LED7, LED6 and LED3 remain ON as well as remaining LEDs are killed.

At t = 4ms: the needle will be at POSITION 5. Same as Position three and four, at this position just LED7, LED6 and LED3 remain ON. Remaining LEDs are killed.

At t = 5ms: the needle will be at POSITION 6. At this position all the 8 LEDs are again fueled on, TOP drove (MSB) to BOTTOM drove (LSB) are turned ON.

At t = 6ms: the needle will be at POSITION 7. Same as Position 6, at this position all the eight LEDs stay on.

As clarified above, we will turn ON suitable LEDs at the fitting Needle Positions to show the fundamental character. On the off chance that the speed of development of needle is moderate we can see each LED section independently. Be that as it may, when the speed of engine is high and needle is moving too quick then the presentation will be viewed as constantly demonstrating "A" character.

Programming Explanation:

We have modified the Arduino to control the proper LED at suitable occasions while pivoting with the goal that LED segment will show the content "CIRCUIT CIRCUIT" in roundabout position.

Programming of the Propeller show is effectively reasonable. A Char Array of 26x8 has been taken as unpredictable scorch ALPHA[26][8]. This Array comprises 8 places of the needle to show every one of the 26 letter sets that makes it cluster of 26x8. 26 pushes in Array speak to the 26 letters in order and 8 sections in each column speak to the eight position of needle to show the character while pivoting. Presently every cell comprise a paired number which speaks to the on/off status of 8 LEDs in a specific situation of Needle. Keep in mind needle here alludes to line of 8 LEDs associated with Arduino as clarified previously.

Presently you simply need to turn the DC engine and utilize a 'for circle' with eight cycles to show a character. Like in the event that you need to show 10 characters, at that point you have to run 10 'for circles' with eight emphasess in each. So we have utilized 13 for circles to show the content CIRCUIT CIRCUIT.
So this is the manner by which you can make a delightful Persistence of Vision (POV) dream with Arduino like a Text is pivoting like a Propeller.

Code

volatile   char   ALPHA[26]

```
[8]={{0,0b01111111,0b11111111,0b11001100,0b1
1001100,0b11001100,0b11111111,0b01111111},

{0,0b00111100,0b01111110,0b11011011,0b11011
011,0b11011011,0b11111111,0b11111111},

{0,0b11000011,0b11000011,0b11000011,0b11000
011,0b11100111,0b01111110,0b00111100},

{0,0b01111110,0b10111101,0b11000011,0b11000
011,0b11000011,0b11111111,0b11111111},

{0,0b11011011,0b11011011,0b11011011,0b11011
011,0b11011011,0b11111111,0b11111111},

{0,0b11011000,0b11011000,0b11011000,0b11011
000,0b11011000,0b11111111,0b11111111},

{0b00011111,0b11011111,0b11011000,0b110110
11,0b11011011,0b11011011,0b11111111,0b1111
1111},

{0,0b11111111,0b11111111,0b00011000,0b00011
000,0b00011000,0b11111111,0b11111111},

{0b11000011,0b11000011,0b11000011,0b111111
11,0b11111111,0b11000011,0b11000011,0b1100
0011},

{0b11000000,0b11000000,0b11000000,0b111111
```

11,0b11111111,0b11000011,0b11001111,0b1100
1111},

{0,0b11000011,0b11100111,0b01111110,0b00111
100,0b00011000,0b11111111,0b11111111},

{0b00000011,0b00000011,0b00000011,0b000000
11,0b00000011,0b00000011,0b11111111,0b1111
1111},

{0b11111111,0b11111111,0b01100000,0b011100
00,0b01110000,0b01100000,0b11111111,0b1111
1111},

{0b11111111,0b11111111,0b00011100,0b001110
00,0b01110000,0b11100000,0b11111111,0b1111
1111},

{0b01111110,0b11111111,0b11000011,0b110000
11,0b11000011,0b11000011,0b11111111,0b0111
1110},

{0,0b01110000,0b11111000,0b11001100,0b11001
100,0b11001100,0b11111111,0b11111111},

{0b01111110,0b11111111,0b11001111,0b110111
11,0b11011011,0b11000011,0b11111111,0b0111
1110},

{0b01111001,0b11111011,0b11011111,0b110111

10,0b11011100,0b11011000,0b11111111,0b1111
1111},

{0b11001110,0b11011111,0b11011011,0b110110
11,0b11011011,0b11011011,0b11111011,0b0111
0011},

{0b11000000,0b11000000,0b11000000,0b111111
11,0b11111111,0b11000000,0b11000000,0b0000
0000},

{0b11111110,0b11111111,0b00000011,0b000000
11,0b00000011,0b00000011,0b11111111,0b1111
1110},

{0b11100000,0b11111100,0b00011110,0b000000
11,0b00000011,0b00011110,0b11111100,0b1110
0000},

{0b11111110,0b11111111,0b00000011,0b111111
11,0b11111111,0b00000011,0b11111111,0b1111
1110},

{0b01000010,0b11100111,0b01111110,0b001111
00,0b00111100,0b01111110,0b11100111,0b0100
0010},

{0b01000000,0b11100000,0b01110000,0b001111
11,0b00111111,0b01110000,0b11100000,0b0100
0000},

```
{0b11000011,0b11100011,0b11110011,0b111110
11,0b11011111,0b11001111,0b11000111,0b1100
0011}};


void setup()
{
  DDRD = 0xFF;
  //a,b,c,d,e,f,g,...z
}
void loop()
{
  for (int i = 7;i > 0;i--)
  {
   PORTD = ALPHA[2][i];
   delay(1);
   PORTD=0;
  }
  delay(2);
  for (int i = 7;i > 0;i--)
  {
   PORTD = ALPHA[8][i];
   delay(1);
   PORTD=0;
  }
```

```
delay(2);
for (int i = 7;i > 0;i--)
{
 PORTD = ALPHA[17][i];
 delay(1);
 PORTD=0;
}
delay(2);
for (int i = 7;i > 0;i--)
{
 PORTD = ALPHA[2][i];
 delay(1);
 PORTD=0;
}
delay(2);
for (int i = 7;i > 0;i--)
{
 PORTD = ALPHA[20][i];
 delay(1);
 PORTD=0;
}
delay(2);
for (int i = 7;i > 0;i--)
{
 PORTD = ALPHA[8][i];
 delay(1);
 PORTD=0;
}
delay(2);
for (int i = 7;i > 0;i--)
```

```
{
 PORTD = ALPHA[19][i];
 delay(1);
 PORTD=0;
}
delay(2);
for (int i = 7;i > 0;i--)
{
 PORTD = ALPHA[3][i];
 delay(1);
 PORTD=0;
}
delay(2);
for (int i = 7;i > 0;i--)
{
 PORTD = ALPHA[8][i];
 delay(1);
 PORTD=0;
}
delay(2);
for (int i = 7;i > 0;i--)
{
 PORTD = ALPHA[6][i];
 delay(1);
 PORTD=0;
}
delay(2);
for (int i = 7;i > 0;i--)
{
 PORTD = ALPHA[4][i];
```

```
  delay(1);
  PORTD=0;
}
delay(2);
for (int i=7;i>0;i--)
{
  PORTD = ALPHA[18][i];
  delay(1);
  PORTD=0;
}
delay(2);
for (int i=7;i>0;i--)
{
  PORTD = ALPHA[19][i];
  delay(1);
  PORTD=0;
}
  delay(19);
}
```

◆ ◆ ◆

10. ADVANCED CELL CONTROLLED HOME AUTOMATION USING ARDUINO

Mechanization is the embodiment of the present world. Computerization can make our life simple and secure. There are numerous approaches to acquire computerization. Computerization can be accomplished by Wi-Fi, IR, GSM, Bluetooth and numerous different innovations.

Beforehand we have secured numerous sorts of Home mechanizations utilizing various advancements like:

- DTMF Based Home Automation

- GSM Based Home Automation utilizing Arduino

- PC Controlled Home Automation utilizing Arduino

- Bluetooth Controlled Home Automation utilizing 8051

- IR Remote Controlled Home Automation utilizing Arduino

- home mechanization undertaking utilizing MATLAB and Arduino

- RF Remote Controlled LEDs Using Raspberry Pi

In this task we are to going to remotely Control Home Appliances utilizing Bluetooth and Arduino. We will tell here that the best way to control electric machines by just sending information from Android Smart telephone to Arduino.

Required Components:

- Arduino Mega (any model)

- Android Phone
- HC05 Bluetooth Modules
- Bluetooth terminal App
- L293D IC
- Two 6V relays
- Two bulbs
- Breadboards
- 12 v, 1A Adapter
- 16x2 LCD

Circuit Diagram:

Circuit outline of this Bluetooth controlled Home Automation is straightforward and associations can be made effectively. LCD, Bluetooth Module HC05 and L293D Driver IC are associated with Arduino.

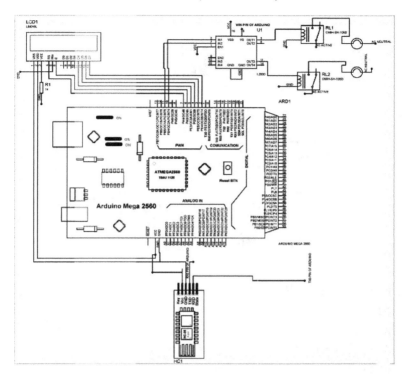

Two Relays are associated with L293D to work two AC machines. Hand-off has all out five pins, in which two pins (around the COM stick) are associated with L293D and GND. Furthermore, COM (normal) Pin is associated with AC mains Live terminal and NO (Normally Open) stick of Relay is associated with one terminal of the Bulb. Other terminal of the bulb is associated with Neutral of AC mains. Check here the working of Relay.

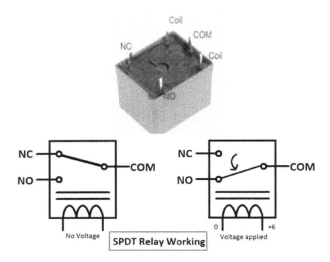

SPDT Relay Working

L293D driver IC is commonly used to expand the momentum. The Vcc2 or VS stick of L293D ought to be associated with VIN stick (input voltage stick or Vcc) of Arduino. Info 1 and Input 2 pins of IC are associated with 10 and 11 stick of Arduino and yield pins are associated with transfers pins.

Working Explanation:

First we have to download and introduce the bluetooth terminal application in our android telephone from the play store as well as afterward pair it with Bluetooth Module HC05 like we typically pair two bluetooth gadgets further check this article arranging bluetooth terminal application for arduino.

Presently we have Bluetooth Terminal App introduced in our Android telephone through which we can send information to Bluetooth Module HC05. HC05 Bluetooth Module is associated with Arduino Mega to sequentially get the information sent by Bluetooth terminal App through Android Smart Phone. A 16x2 LCD is utilized to show the On as well as Off status of Electronic Appliances. What's more, L293D IC is utilized to drive two Relay which are legitimately associated with two Bulbs. 12v Adapter is utilized to control the Arduino and the circuit.

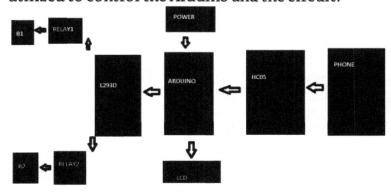

At whatever point we send information by Android telephone, Arduino checks for the character sent and puts suitable sticks high or low as per Code. These pins control the transfers which in turns control the Appliances. The activity of our undertaking is as per the following:

- On the off chance that we send 'a' through Bluetooth Terminal App then Bulb1 will be On and Bulb2 will be off.

- On the off chance that we send 'b' through bluetooth terminal application then bulb2 will be on as well as bulb1 will be off.

- On the off chance that we send 'c' through Bluetooth Terminal App then both the bulbs will be turned On.

- In the event that we send 'd' through bluetooth terminal application then both the bulbs will be turned Off. character 'd' can be utilized to turn off individual bulbs as well.

You can learn here increasingly about Arduino hand-off control.

Programming Explanation:

Program for this Project is straightforward and can be effectively reasonable.

Incorporate LiquidCrystal.h header document in your Arduino Code, it is vital for working of LCD.

```
#include <LiquidCrystal.h>

LiquidCrystal lcd(7, 6, 5, 4, 3, 2);
```

Arrange stick 11 and 10 as yield pins of Arduino as

beneath in void arrangement() capacity and use Serial.begin(9600) for correspondence among Arduino and Android telephone by means of Bluetooth Module HC05.

```
void setup() {

    pinMode(11, OUTPUT);

    pinMode(10, OUTPUT);

    Serial.begin(9600);

    lcd.begin(16, 2);

    lcd.print("**AUTOMATION**");

}
```

In void circle() work, check for the nearness of any sequential information and put that information in a variable roast c.

```
void loop() {

    if (Serial.available() > 0)

    {
```

```
char c = Serial.read();

if(c == 'a')

{

Serial.print("in a code");

.........

.........
```

At that point think about that sequential information (scorch c) with character 'a' ,'b', 'c', 'd', which is sent by Android Smart Phone by client. Subsequent to contrasting, Arduino will turn on or off the Appliances as indicated by our different conditions in our Code. You can change the code as indicated by your prerequisite. Check the full code underneath.

Code

```
#include <LiquidCrystal.h>
LiquidCrystal lcd(7, 6, 5, 4, 3, 2);
void setup() {
 pinMode(11, OUTPUT);
 pinMode(10, OUTPUT);
 Serial.begin(9600);
 lcd.begin(16, 2);
 lcd.print("**AUTOMATION**");
```

```
}
void loop() {
 if (Serial.available() > 0)
 {
  char c = Serial.read();
  if (c == 'a')
  {
  Serial.print("in a code");
  digitalWrite(10,HIGH);
  digitalWrite(11,LOW);
  Serial.print("10 HIGH");
  lcd.clear();
  lcd.print("**BULB1 ON**");
  }

   if(c=='b')
  {
  digitalWrite(11,HIGH);
  digitalWrite(10,LOW);
  Serial.print("11 HIGH");
  lcd.clear();
  lcd.print("**BULB2 ON**");
  }

   if(c=='c')
  {
  digitalWrite(10,HIGH);
  digitalWrite(11,HIGH);
  lcd.clear();
```

```
  lcd.print("**BULB 1,2 ON**");
  }


   if(c=='d')
  {
  digitalWrite(10,LOW);
  digitalWrite(11,LOW);
  lcd.clear();
  lcd.print("**BULB 1,2 OFF**");
  }
 }
}
```

THANK YOU !!!